Roschkov

Editorial Cartoons

Introduction by Gary Lautens

Prentice-Hall of Canada, Ltd., Scarborough, Ontario

Canadian Cataloguing in Publication Data

Roschkov, Vic, 1941 —
    Roschkov editorial cartoons

ISBN 0-13-783316-4

1. Editorial cartoons. 2. Canadian wit and humor,
Pictorial. I. Title.

NC1449.R68A4 1979   741.5'971   C79-094551-7

© 1979 by Prentice-Hall of Canada, Ltd., Scarborough, Ontario
All Rights Reserved. No part of this book may be reproduced in any
form or by any means without permission in writing from the publisher.

Cartoons reproduced with the permission of the *Toronto Star* and the
Windsor Star.

Prentice-Hall, Inc., Englewood Cliffs, New Jersey
Prentice-Hall International, Inc., London
Prentice-Hall of Australia, Pty., Ltd., Sydney
Prentice-Hall of India, Pvt., Ltd., New Delhi
Prentice-Hall of Japan, Inc., Tokyo
Prentice-Hall of Southeast Asia (Pte.) Ltd., Singapore

ISBN 0-13-783316-4

1 2 3 4 5 W 83 82 81 80 79

Printed and bound in Canada

Introduction

It's always a mistake to write an introduction for a book of political cartoons. People want to get to the drawings themselves; they don't want to spend precious moments over even a paragraph of print when there are dozens of delightful drawings waiting only a page or two away.

All right, let me get down to the business of making the introductions.

The name of the cartoonist is Vic Roschkov, he is 37 years of age, and he lives in the Beaches area of Toronto with his wife Carole-Anne and sons Vic junior, 16, and Tommy, 14. He was born in Kiev, Ukraine, and was tossed around Europe with his family by World War Two, until they left a displaced persons camp in Belgium for Canada in 1950. In this country he's lived in Montreal, North Bay, Windsor, London, Brantford and now Toronto.

What else?

Well, Vic is a grade 10 dropout and he's never had an art lesson in his life. He was a $20-a-week dishwasher, a tobacco-picker and a labourer in a cement factory before he got a job cutting stencils at a silk screen shop. There he talked politics during coffee breaks and did doodles of co-workers. It was by accident that he discovered he could do caricatures. A big surprise, but once onto it he was hooked.

For most of the next two years he did political cartoons in his spare time, compiling a portfolio which he sent around to everyone he thought might be interested. The portfolio got a lot of praise, but no one bought. Vic was ready to quit the pounding when the Canadian edition of *Time Magazine* bought a cartoon featuring Pierre Trudeau and Bob Stanfield.

The *Windsor Star* also agreed to use some of his cartoons and he later moved to the paper as its full-time political cartoonist until lured away in 1976 by the *Toronto Star*.

And that is where he is today—in the next office to mine, in fact, where, if I can interpret the silence, he is at this moment staring out his window at Lake Ontario, or the CN Tower, puffing on his pipe, and trying to shape today's idea and put it on paper.

Let me quickly fill in a few more details before your patience is totally exhausted. Vic (who looks a little like George the Fifth or a good natural czar) fishes, reads and shoots pool in his spare time. Occasionally he gets additional exercise by throwing things like paste pots across his office, especially when the reproduction of one of his drawings isn't up to his standard. He must own a suit, good shirt and necktie, but I've never seen him dressed that way—only in slacks, casual shirt and sweater. He has absolutely no airs.

Like all good creative people, he takes his work very seriously, but not himself.

His commitment?

When his passion boils over about deception in public life,

arrogance in high places or violence in hockey the emotion is real. If you met him you'd like him.

His skills?

The hardest part for Vic isn't the drawing, it's coming up with a unique and clever way to make a point. He watches the news closely. He has the insight into that news to recognize its essential comic elements and transform them into humorous drawings. Vic combines insight and artistic talent at their best.

His standards?

His profession is all-consuming. Vic has constantly got one ear at a radio broadcast, one eye on a newspaper and one eye on the TV news. He works in his sleep.

It's true!

This past February 28 Vic did a drawing for the next day's paper. When he finally put down his pens and brushes, it was pretty late in the day, not far from midnight. The only trouble was, Vic wasn't satisfied with his work. But he finally went home when he felt he could do no more.

The next morning I heard the rest of the story.

Around 2 o'clock in the morning, Vic sat bolt upright in bed. While sleeping, or sort of sleeping, it finally hit him that a little extra cross-hatching (plain shading to civilians like you and me) would improve the cartoon.

Vic got dressed, backed out the car and started for the office.

That is not the end of it.

Halfway to the office Vic noticed the ominous flashing light of a police cruiser behind him and he was waved to the curb. The 1979 licence sticker deadline was midnight, and Vic had broken the law by two hours and a few minutes—all because he was such a perfectionist he had to add a few lines to tomorrow's cartoon, and at 2:30 in the morning.

The fine was $28.

Perhaps I should add a postscript.

Vic had bought his 1979 sticker, but it was still at home. He had planned to put it on his licence in the morning before going to work, but worry about his cartoon in the middle of the night had unfortunately driven such practical thoughts from his mind.

Anyway, *Toronto Star* readers and others across the country who saw the cartoon (yes, with the $28 worth of extra shading) undoubtedly never suspected how much trouble Vic Roschkov had gone to in order to give them something just a little bit better.

So here we have the very first collection of Vic Roschkov's cartoons and everyone who knows him, and many who don't, will be delighted at his acute wit and clever satire. What you are about to see is a long, long way from Kiev, the tobacco fields of Ontario, and the grade 10 dropout who didn't know what he was going to do with his life.

Gary Lautens

Roschkov Editorial Cartoons

The New Cultural Revolution

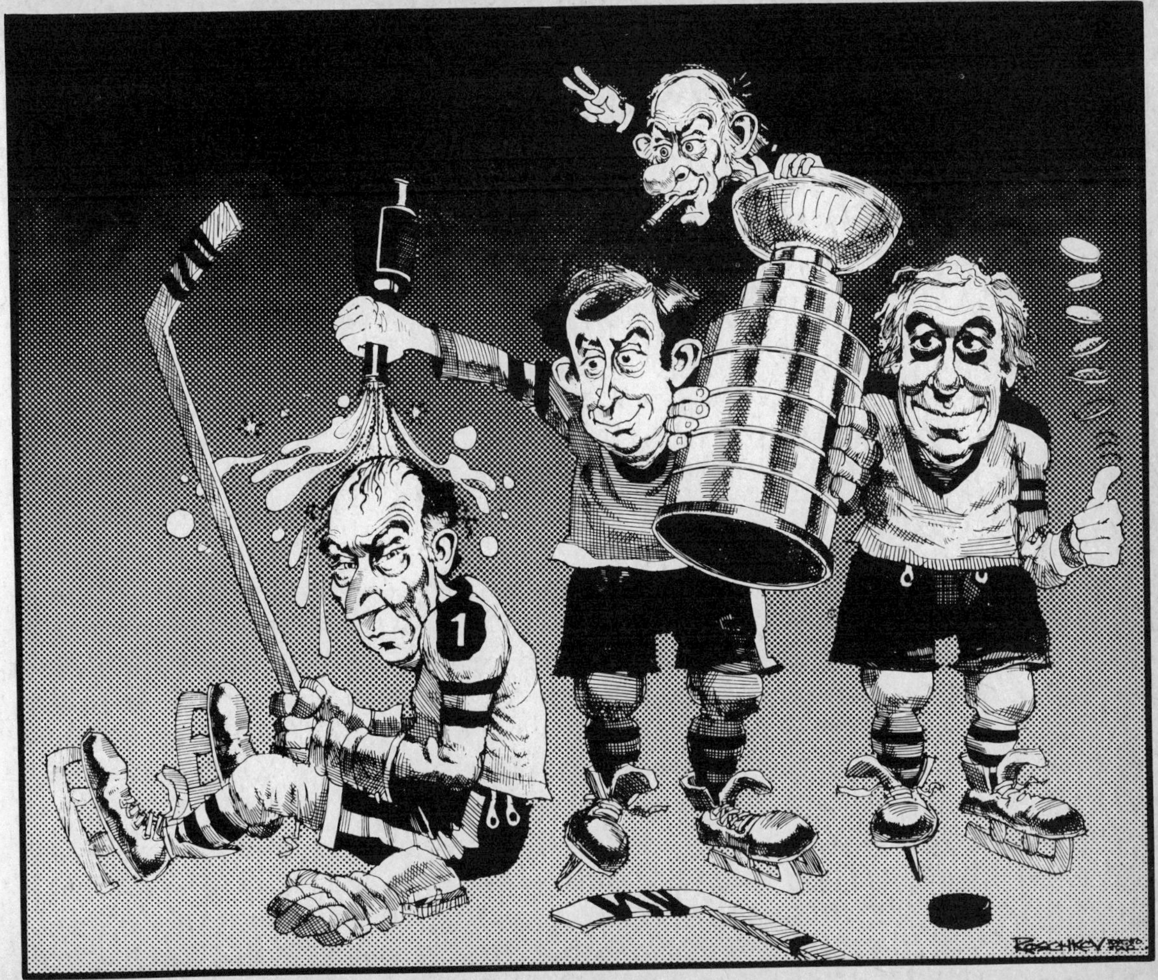

Our International Image

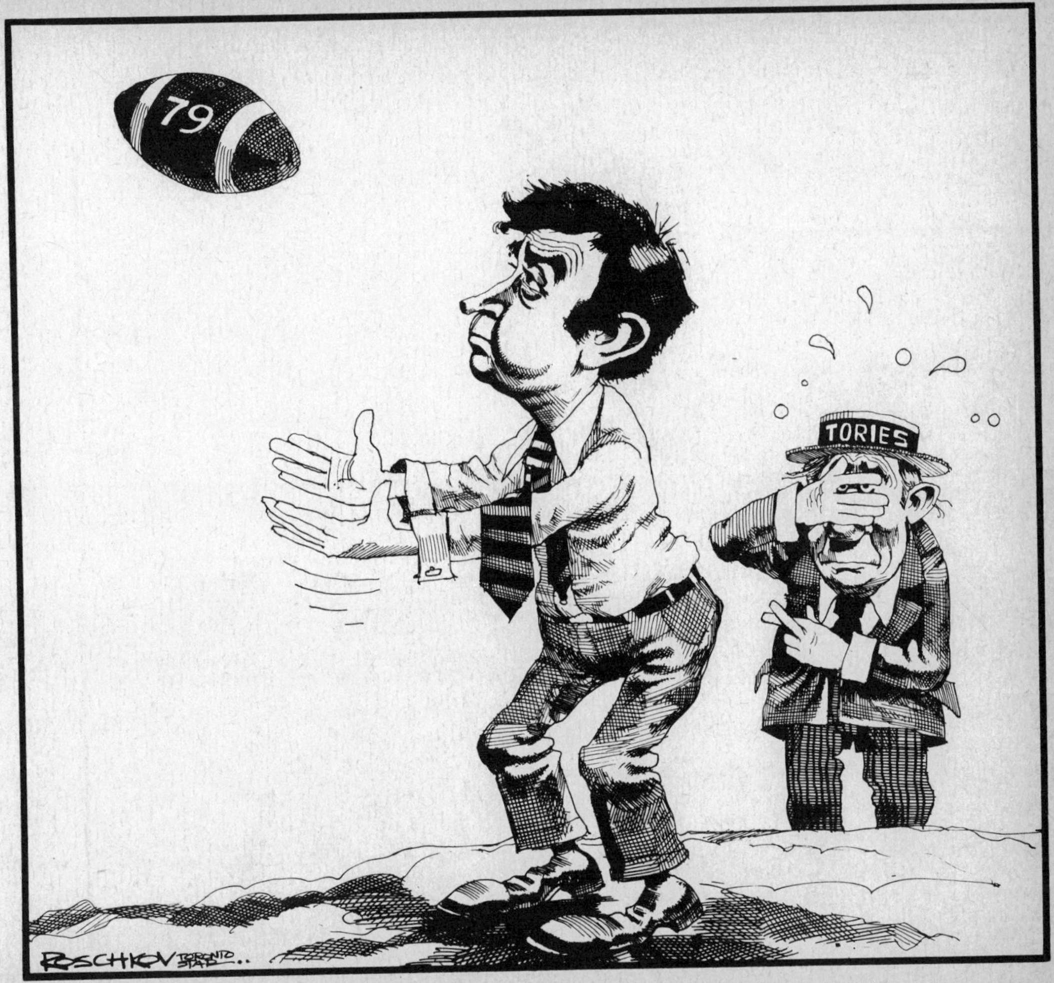
79
TORIES
ROSCHKOV TORONTO STAR

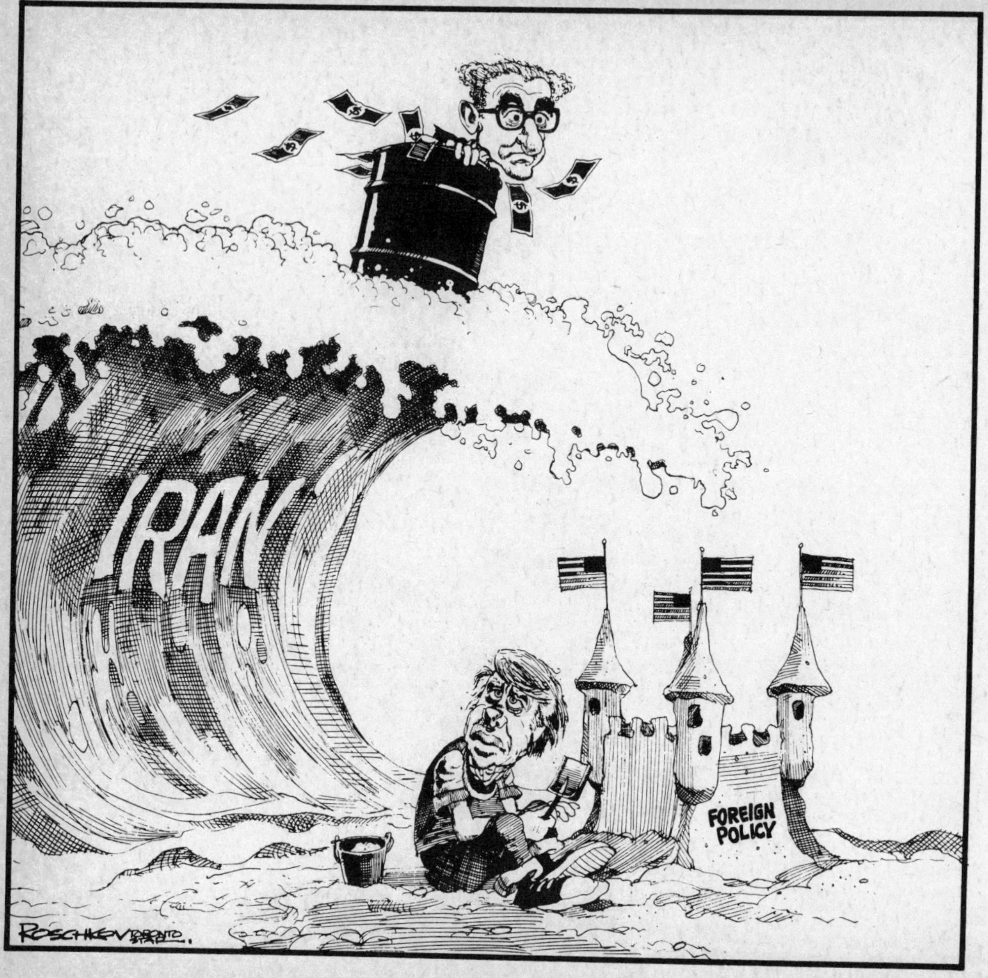
IRAN
FOREIGN POLICY
ROSCHKOV TORONTO STAR

CANADIAN TIRE
Coca-Camille
CHRYSLER
Mclevesque's
ROYAL BANQUE
CHEVROLET
PQ SIGNS
AIR CANADA
7UP
ROSCHKOV TORONTO STAR

People City?

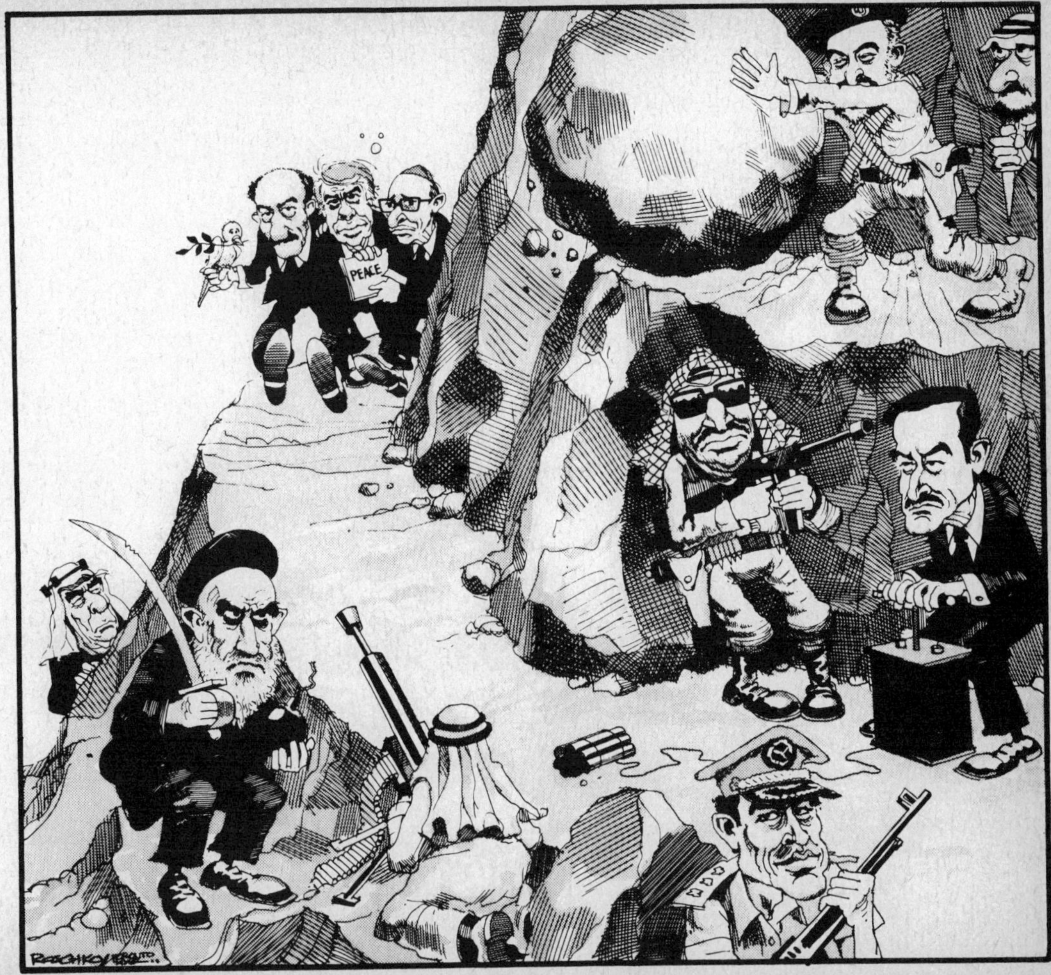
PEACE

MR SPEAKER_ I WISH TO DIRECT A QUESTION TO THE NOBODIES IN THE GOVERNMENT BENCHES
ROSCHKOV
TORONTO STAR

Seasonally Adjusted

A Mission of Peace,
Love and Security for Europe

◀ The Tories can keep this country together . . .

"OK that does it!
No more independence,
common markets, new deals within ▶
confederation—it's back to
separation . . ."

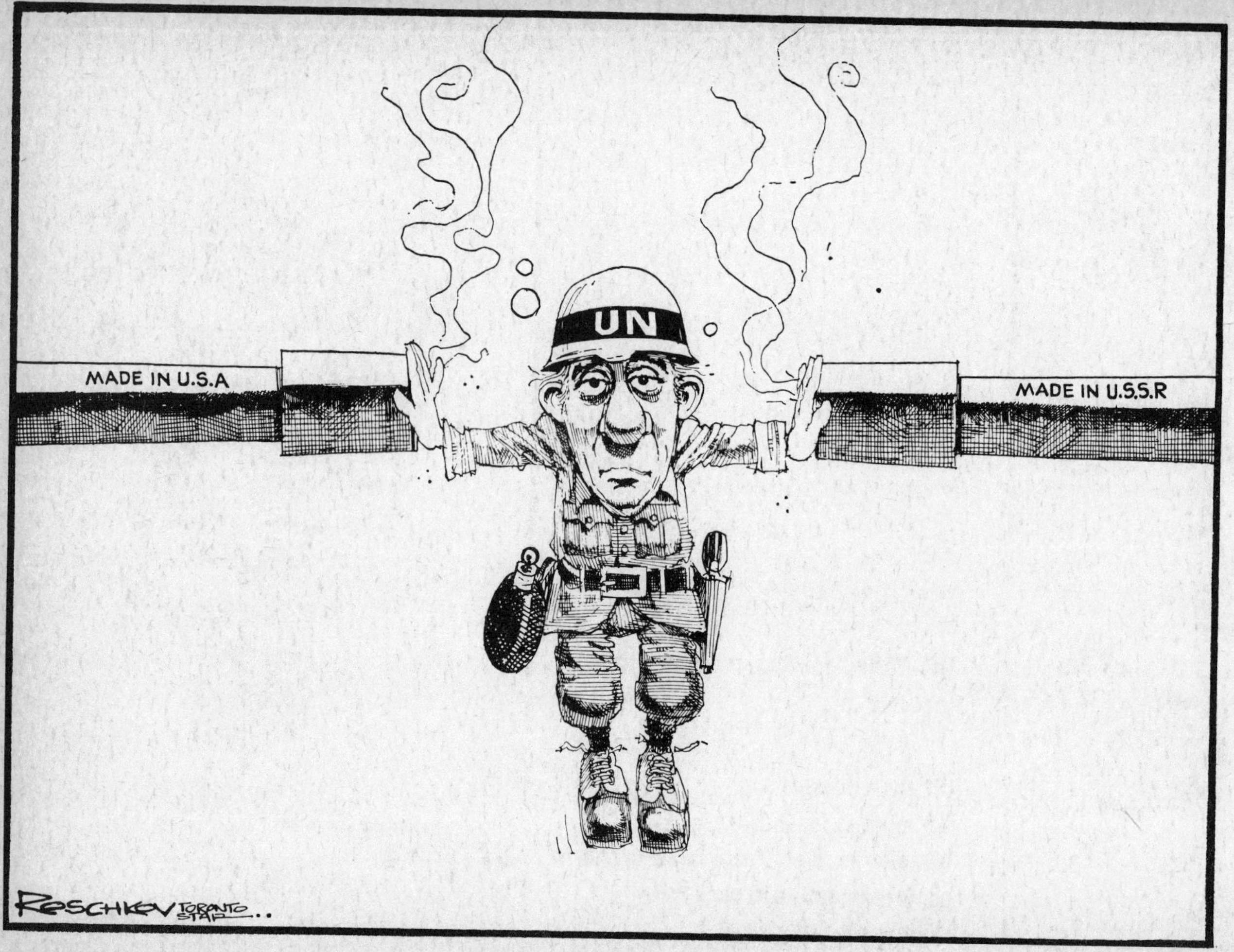
UN
MADE IN U.S.A
MADE IN U.S.S.R
RESCHKOV
TORONTO STAR

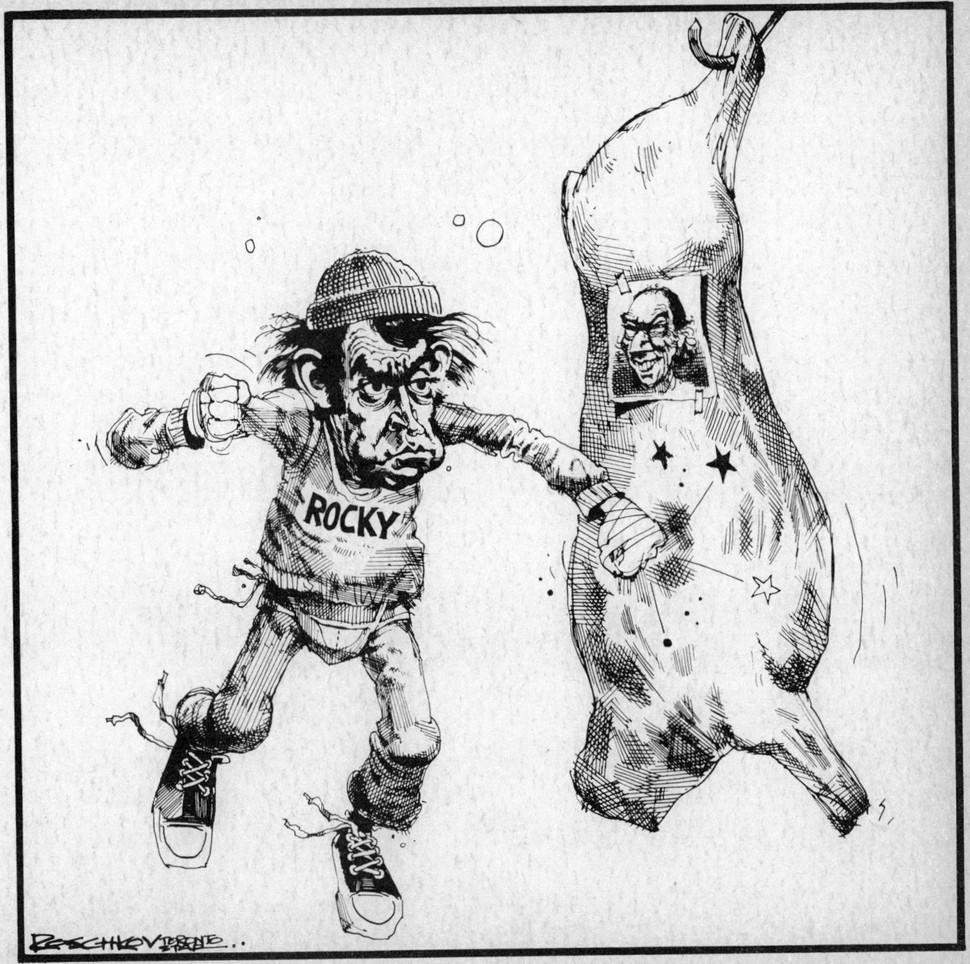
ROCKY

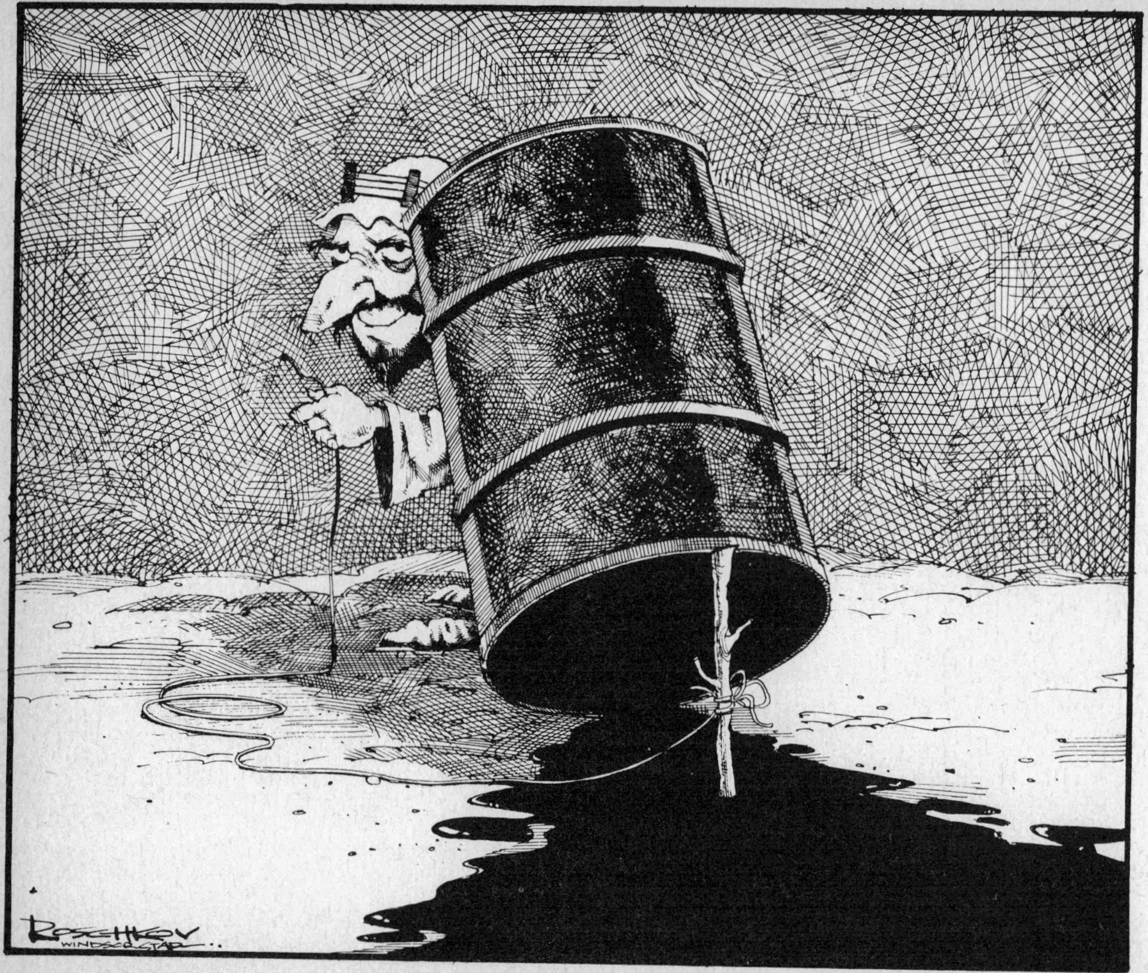
ROSCHKOV

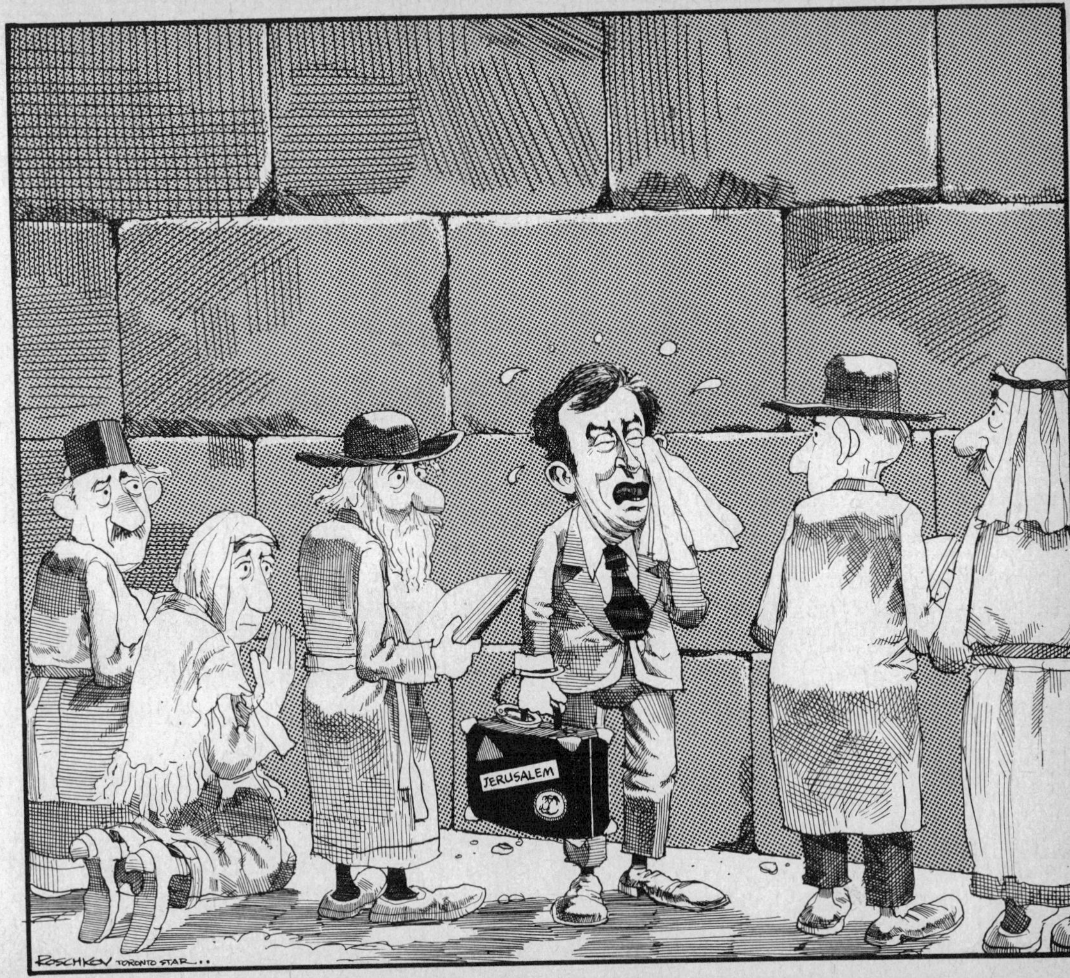
JERUSALEM
ROSCHKOV TORONTO STAR

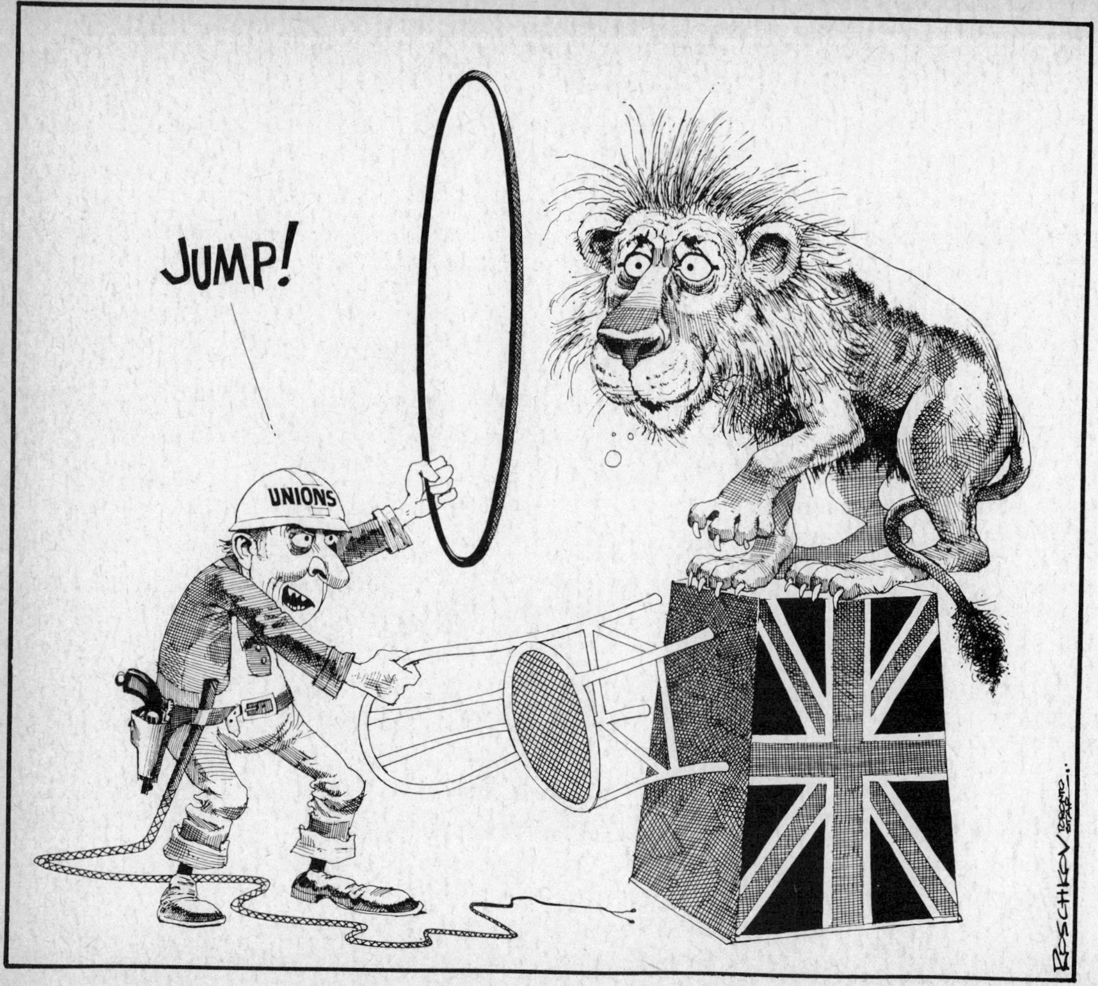
JUMP!
UNIONS
BOSCHKOV
TORONTO STAR

840,000 Unemployed

AHA! THOUGHT I WAS SLEEPING_ EH MOUSE?
JOBS
ROSCHKOV TORONTO STAR

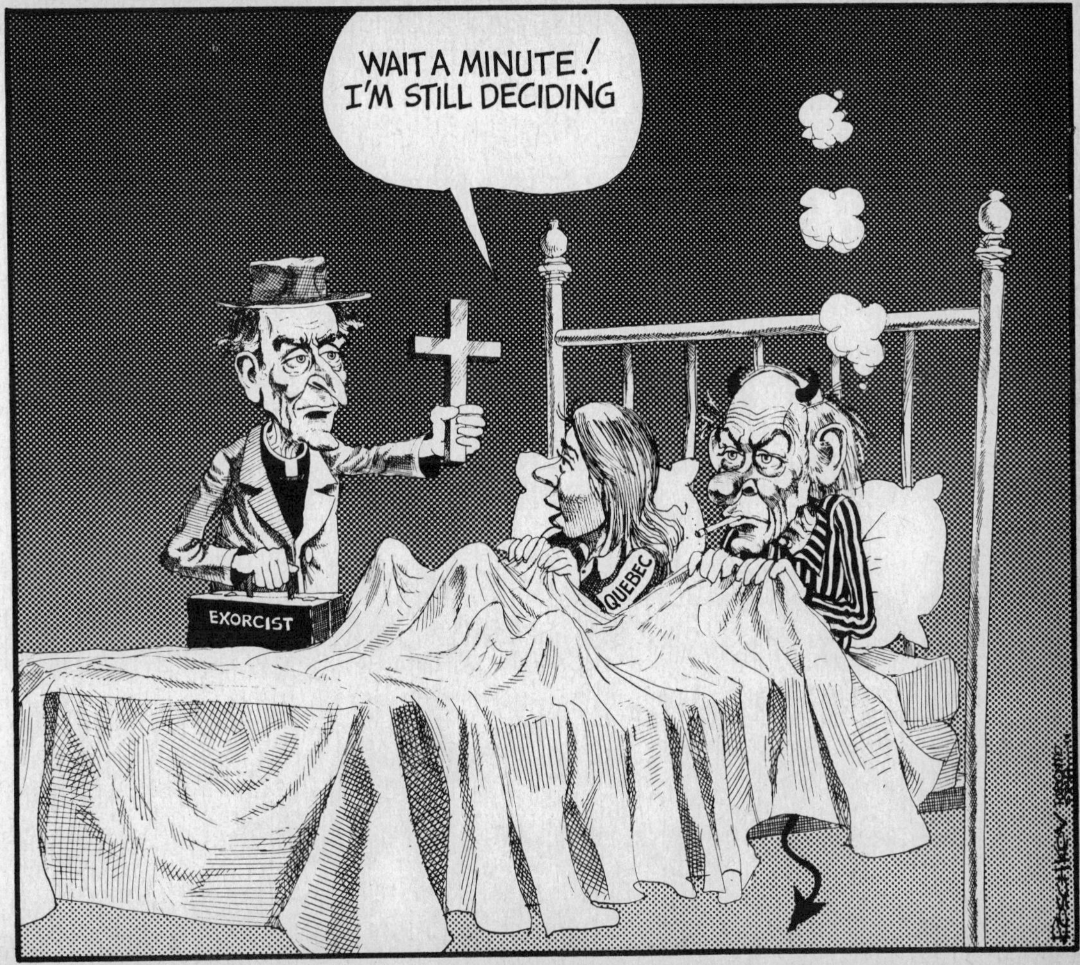
WAIT A MINUTE!
I'M STILL DECIDING
EXORCIST
QUEBEC

Yas, Yas, a New Game in Ontario

DEALER'S CHOICE — THE GAME IS SEPARATION, IT'S PLAYED WITH MY CARDS AND YOUR MONEY
ROSCHKOV

"Send us your technology so we can expand our teaching techniques."

"We've decided to invest it — we'll buy the other nine provinces"

"Okay, okay, don't shoot!"

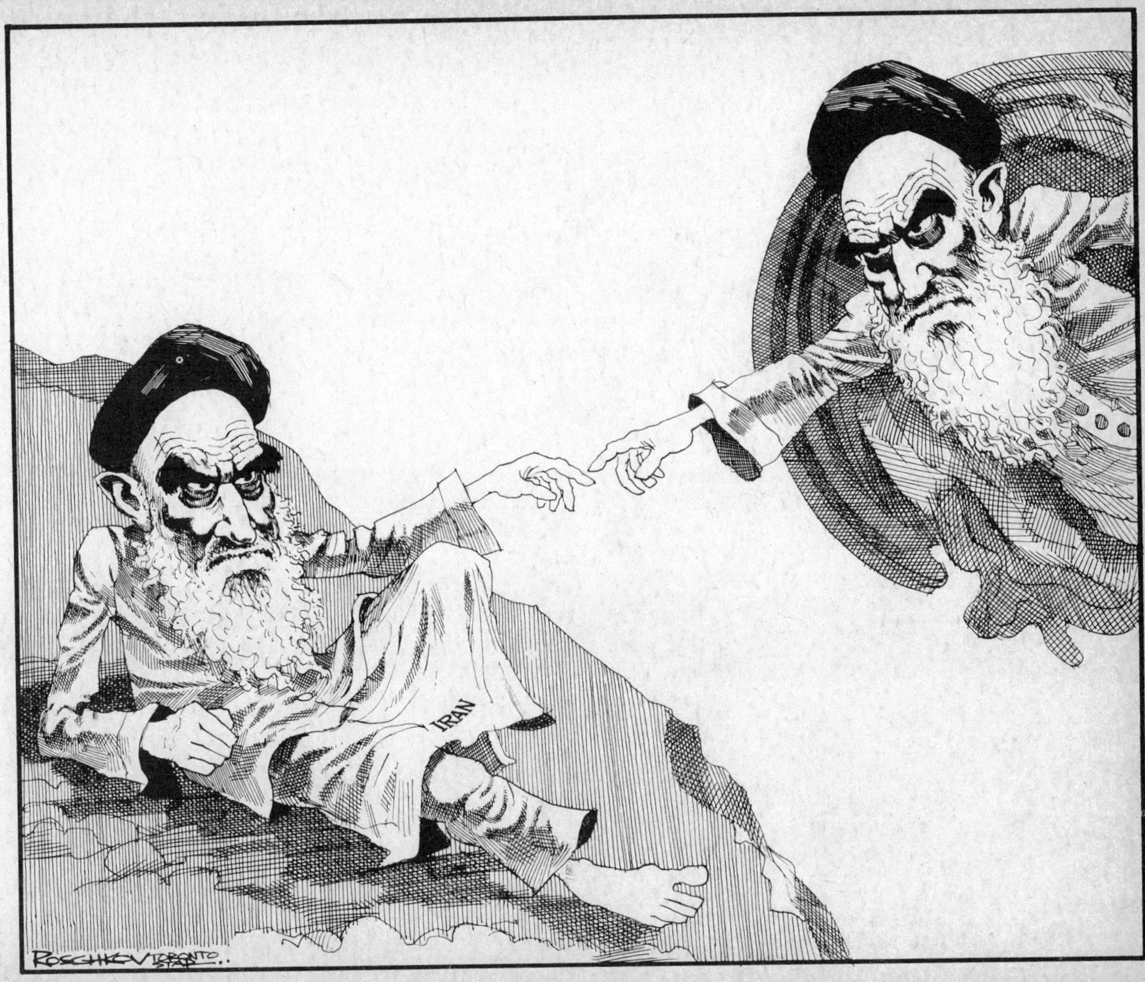
IRAN
ROSCHKOV TORONTO STAR

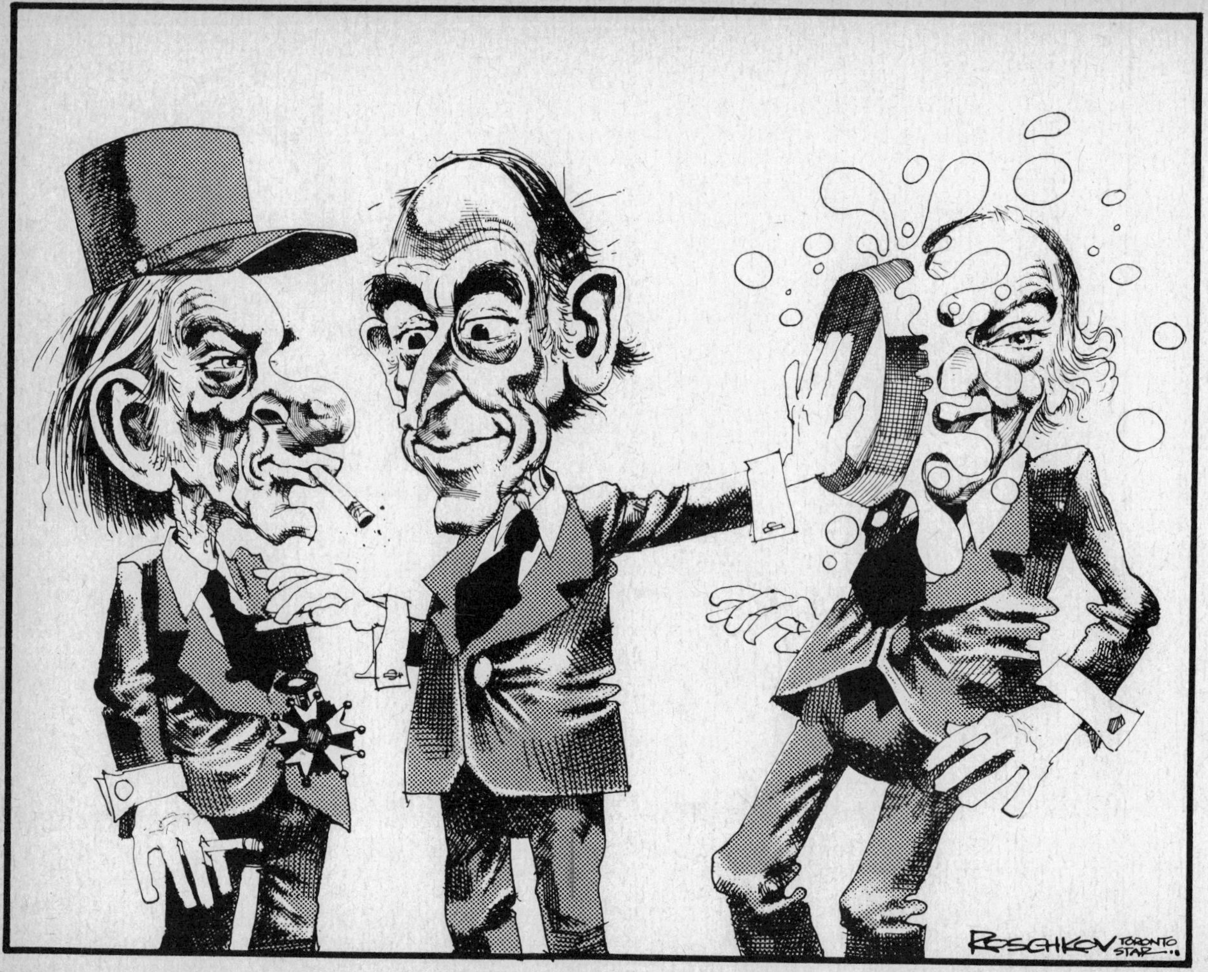
ROSCHKOV
TORONTO STAR

"Ottawa's action during French Premier Barre's visit is typical of a policy systematically designed to put down and humiliate Quebec." RENE LEVESQUE

The Tag Team

"Next!"

PRAVDA
VIETNAM
BONN VOTES TO
KEEP HUNTING
WAR CRIMINALS
ROSCHKOV TORONTO STAR

"Free trade? Splendid idea—you're short of marbles and screws, and we're short of everything..."

Cults

PIERRE'S SUMMIT

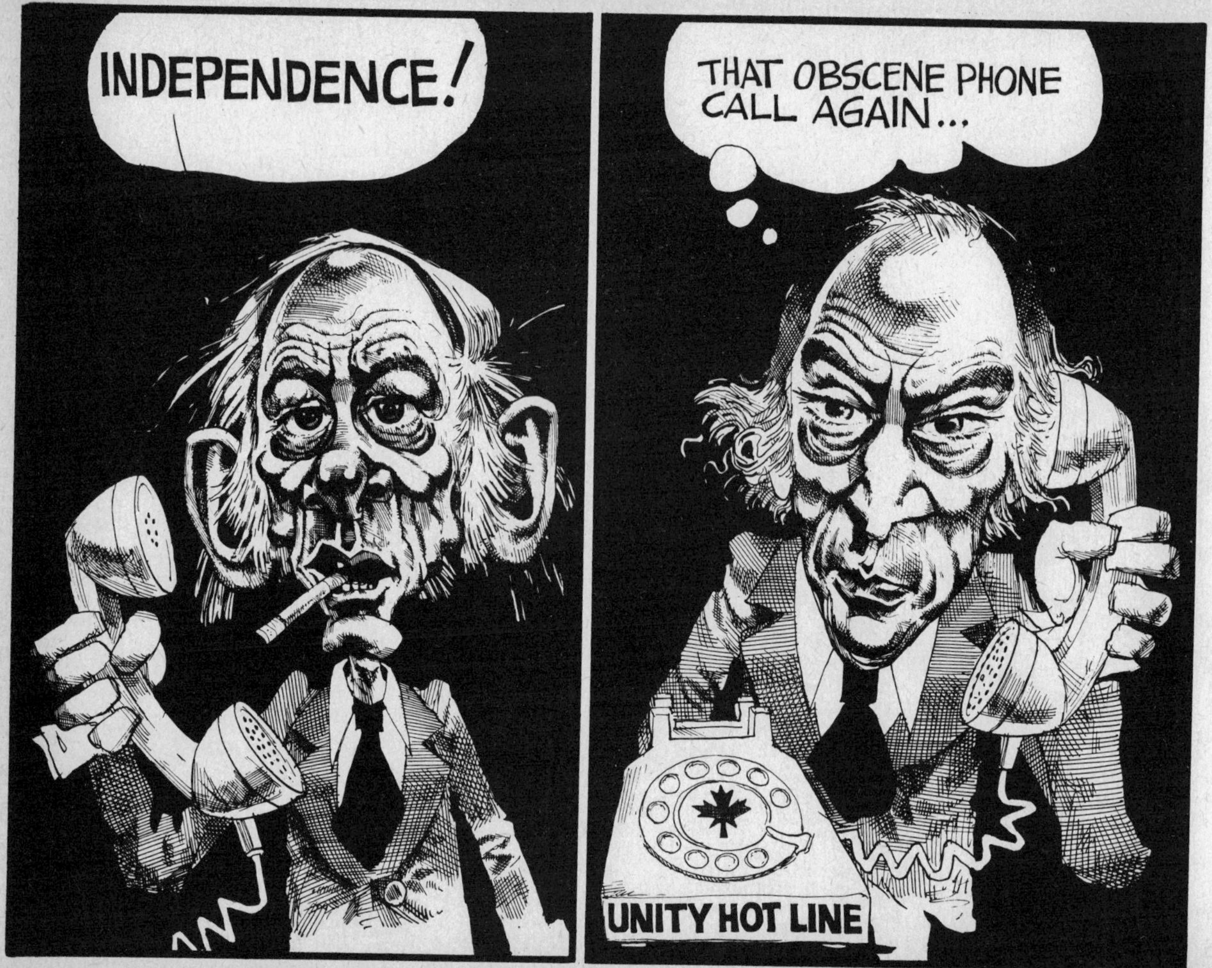
INDEPENDENCE!
THAT OBSCENE PHONE CALL AGAIN...
UNITY HOT LINE

TELEGRAM FROM OPEC—THEY JUST RAISED THEIR PRICES AND PUT THE WORLD ON AN ODD-EVEN SYSTEM
TOKYO SUMMIT
ROSCHKOV TORONTO STAR

World Politics

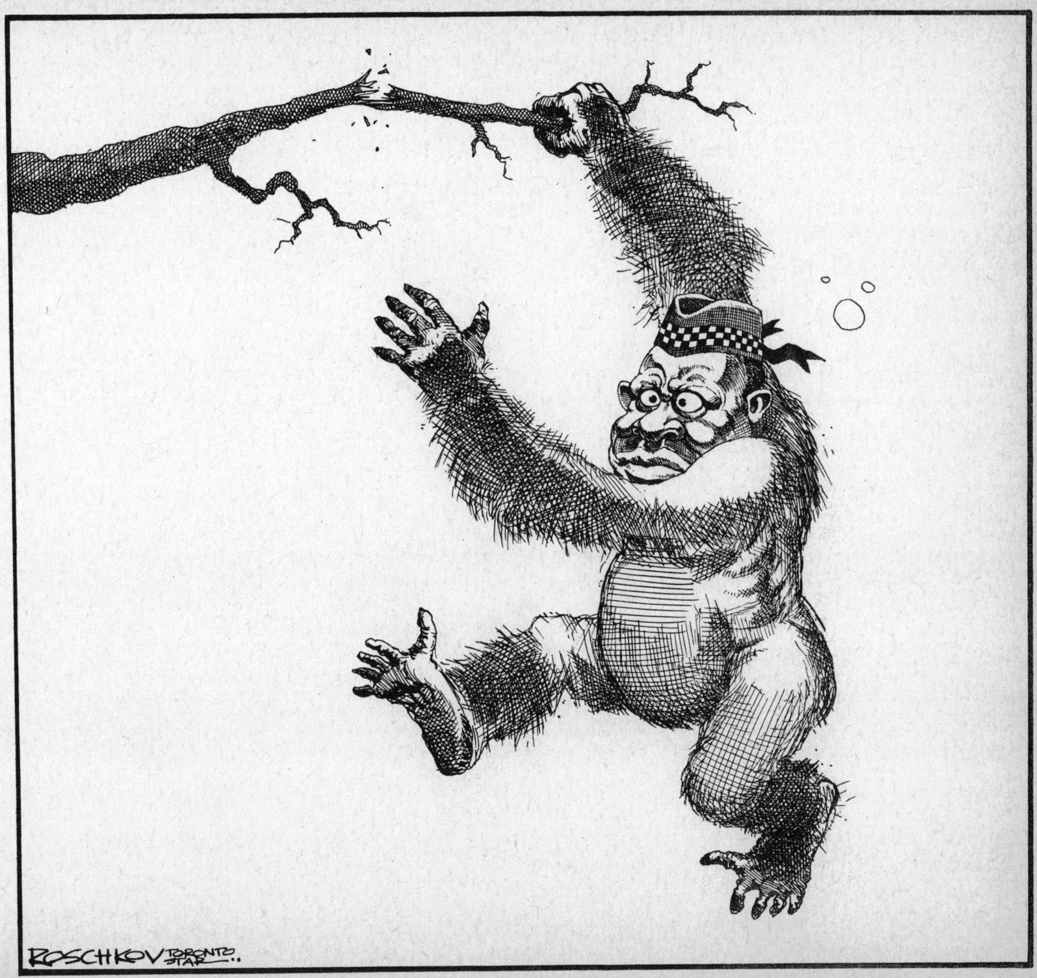
ROSCHKOV TORONTO STAR

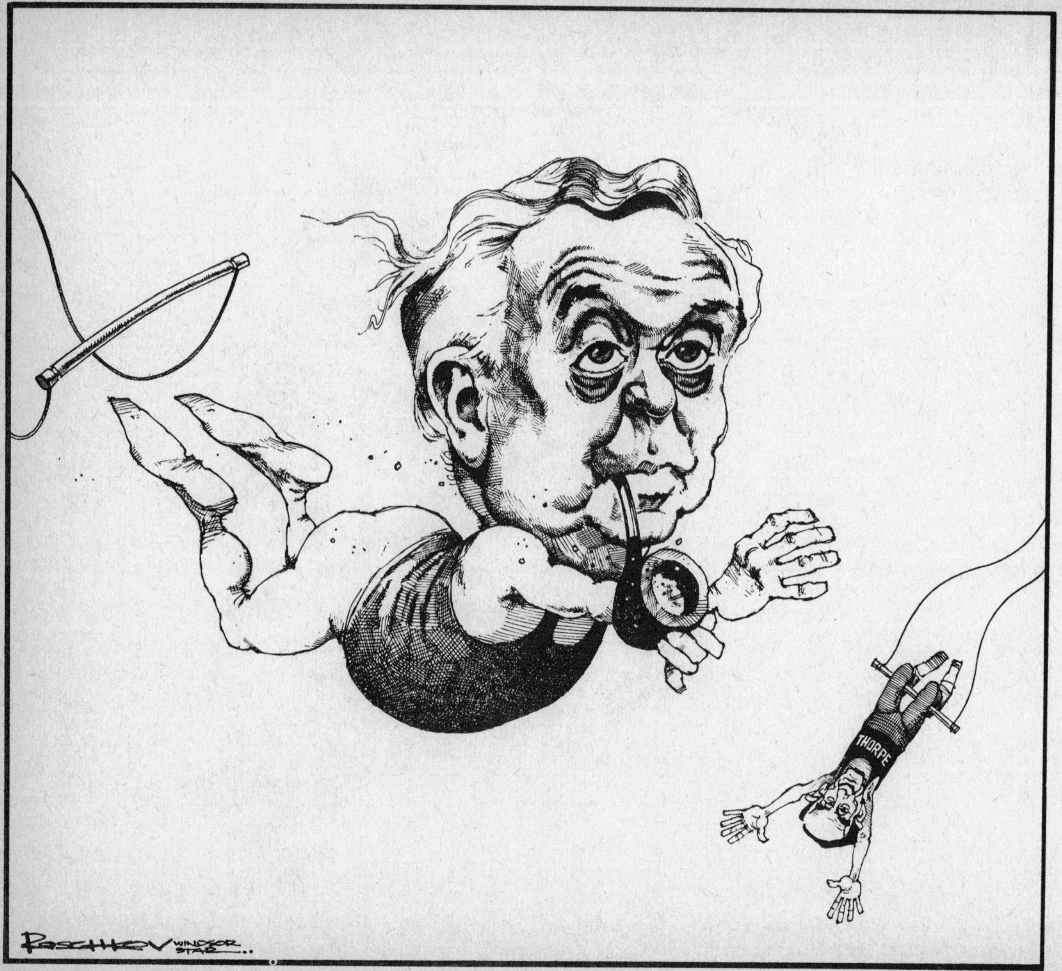
THORPE
WINDSOR STAR

The Superpowers

I'M GOING TO GIVE YOU A CHANCE_WE'LL FINISH THE 15TH ROUND NEXT SPRING
KID FEDERALIST
ROSCHKOV TORONTO STAR

"I have just made a very important discovery—I discovered that we should stop discovering new discoveries and start discovering solutions to the problems caused by our old discoveries."

WHAT DO YA MEAN, SET A GOOD EXAMPLE FOR THE KIDS? WE GOTTA IMPRESS THE NHL BOSSES
NHL
3
ROSCHKOV

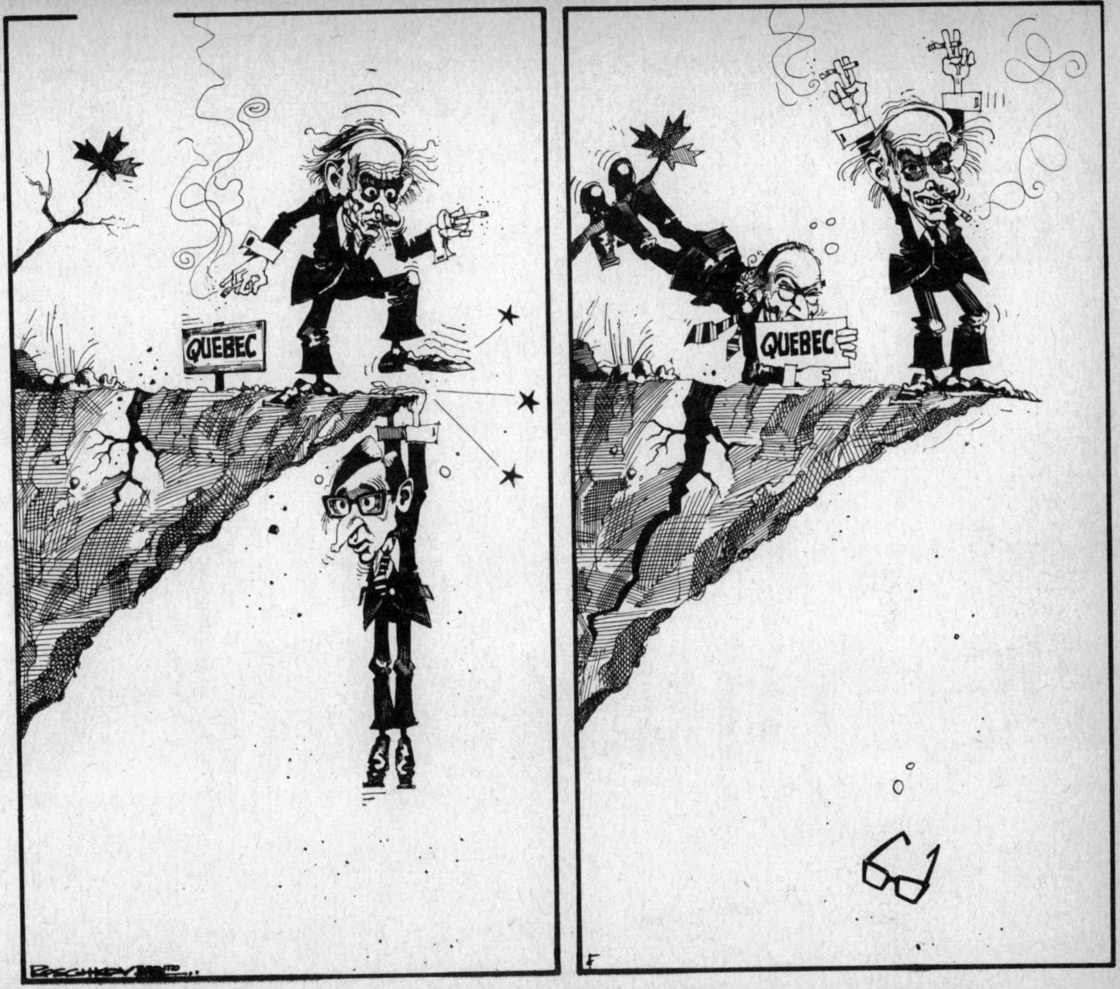
QUEBEC
QUEBEC

IT'S ALCOHOL, A HARMLESS DRUG THAT SHOULD BE LEGALIZED
ROSCHKOV TORONTO STAR

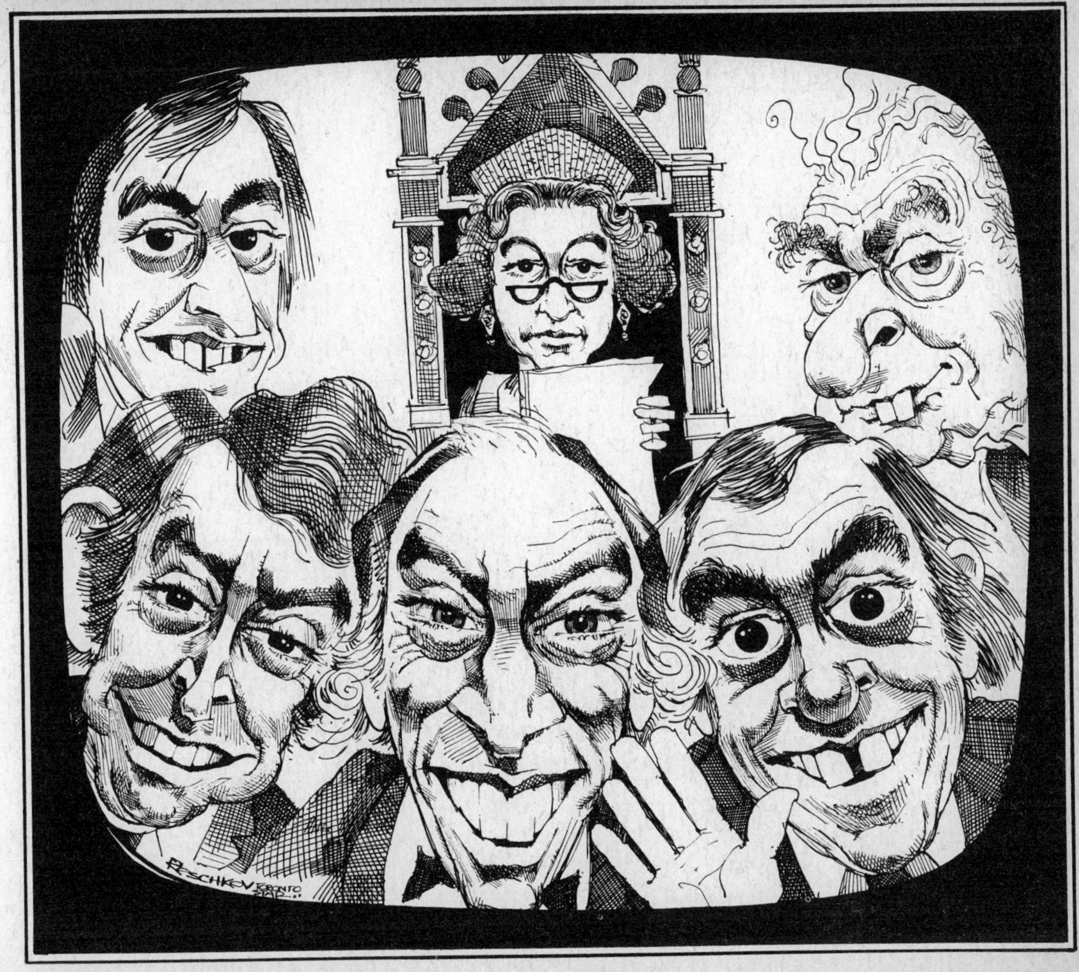
PESCHKOV TORONTO STAR

Political Football in Southeast Asia

NEWS ITEM — P.Q. spies on unions

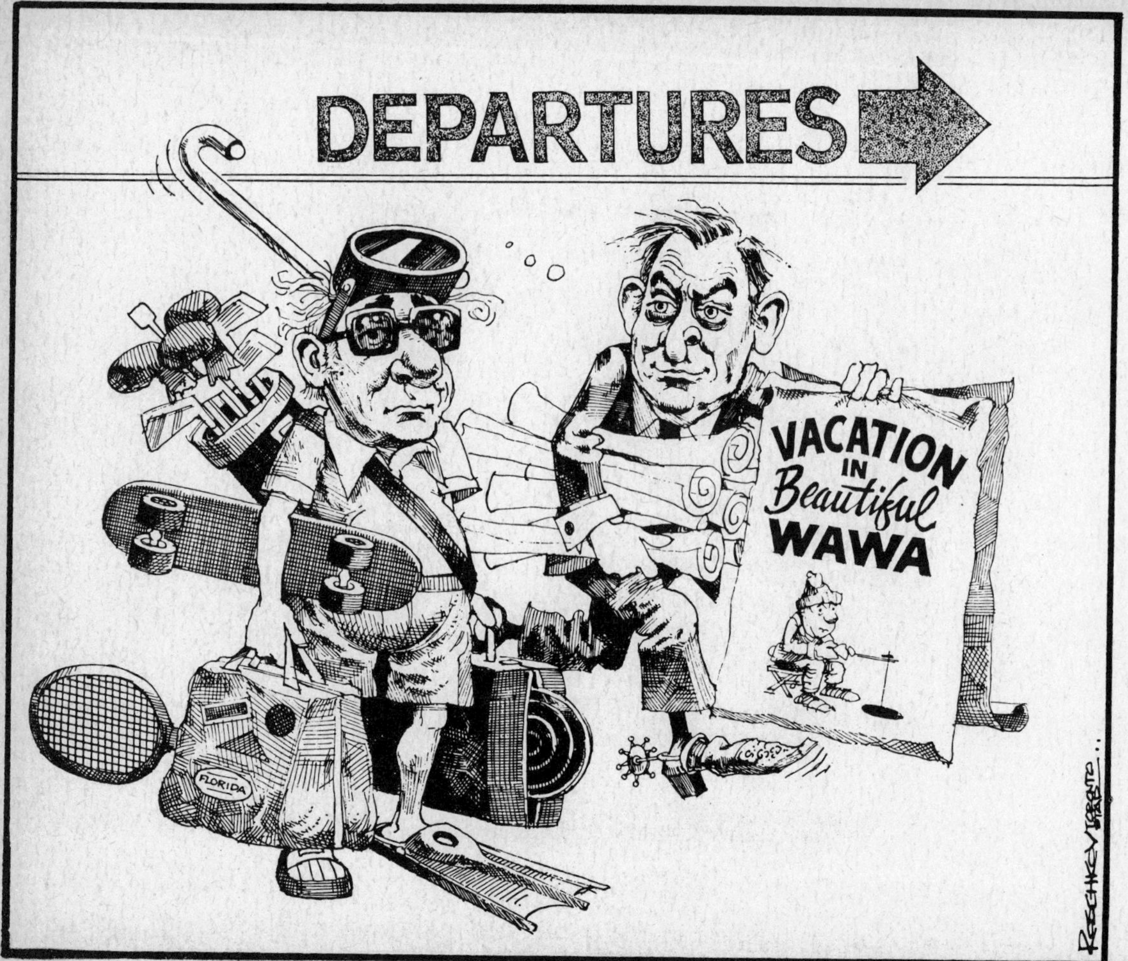
DEPARTURES
VACATION IN Beautiful WAWA
FLORIDA

"If anyone comes ashore—you're Robinson Crusoe and I'm Friday."

"If elected, we promise to be inferior."

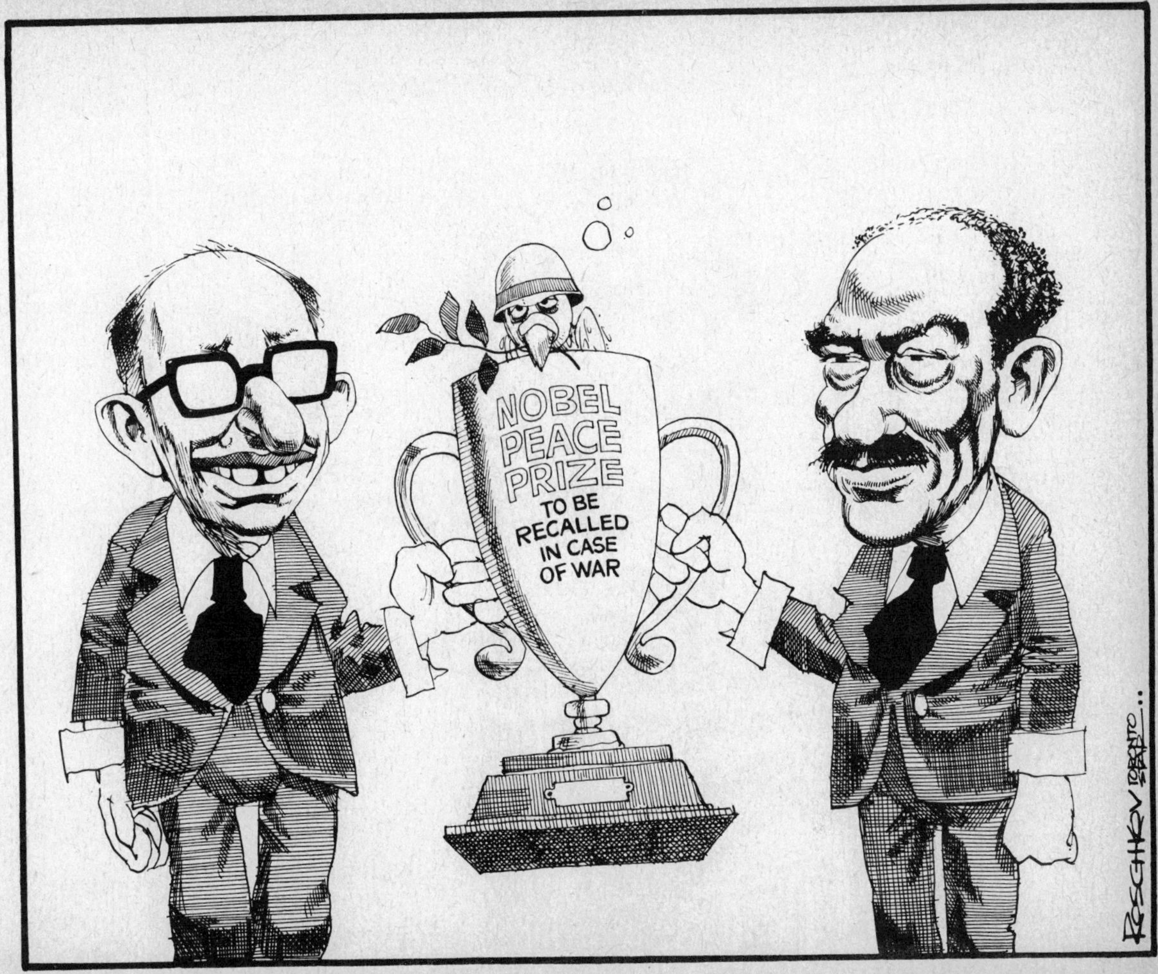
NOBEL
PEACE
PRIZE
TO BE
RECALLED
IN CASE
OF WAR

"—I have come bearing an olive branch and a freedom fighter's gun."

"Do not adjust your set—this is the condition of your country."

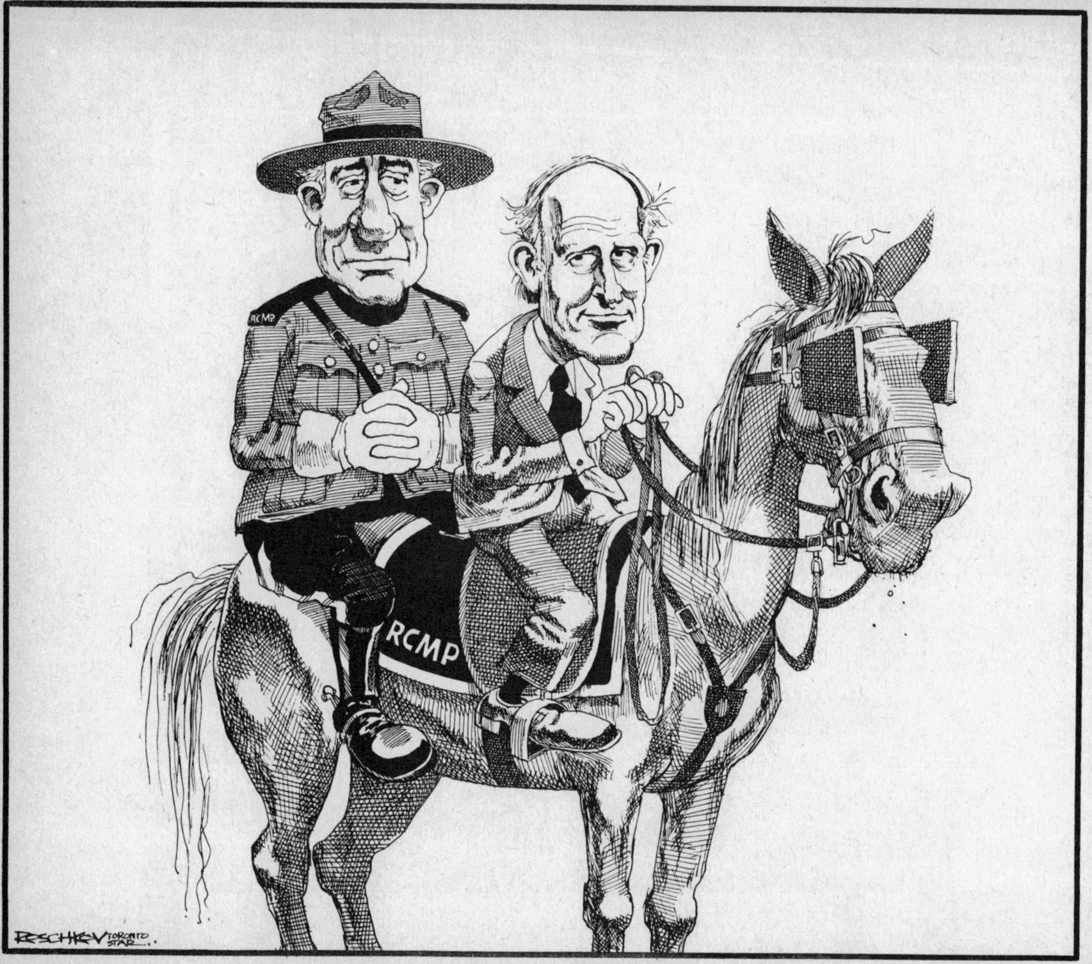
RCMP
RCMP

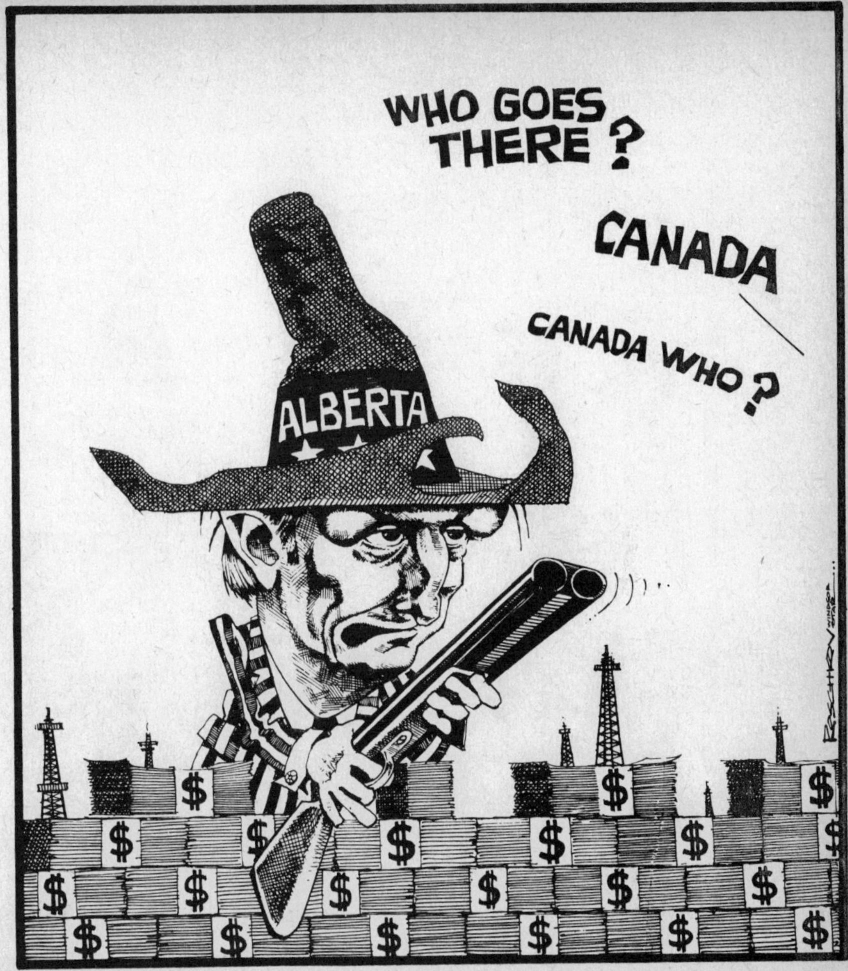
WHO GOES THERE ?
CANADA
CANADA WHO ?
ALBERTA

Economic Policy

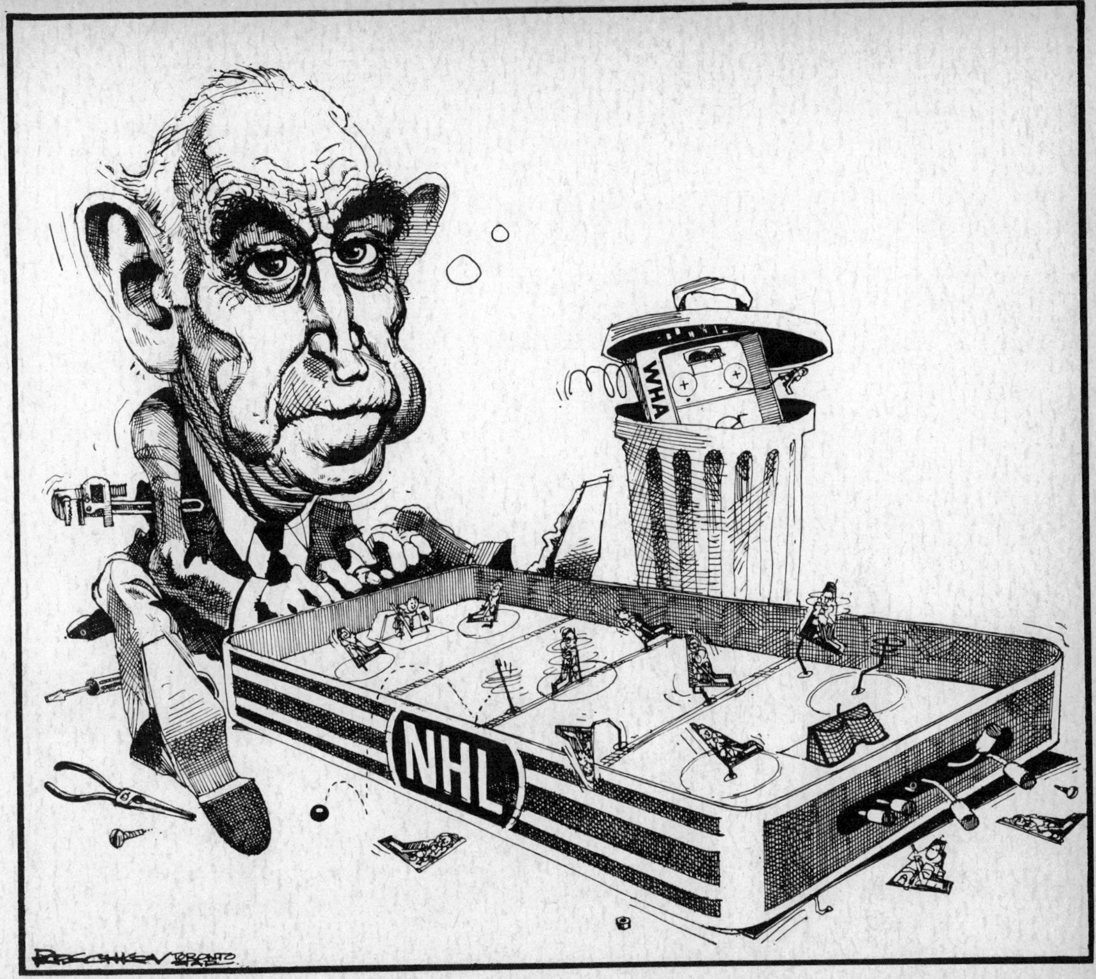
WHA
NHL
REISCHKEV TORONTO STAR

NUDE
RTAINMENT
NO PARKING
EVER
YONGE ST.
BOOKS
ADULT
HERE GOES THE NEIGHBORHOOD
MEANINGFUL NUDE ENCOUNTER UP STAIRS
THE JOY OF FILTH

The Domino Theory

"They're promising the sun—
haven't we already done that?"

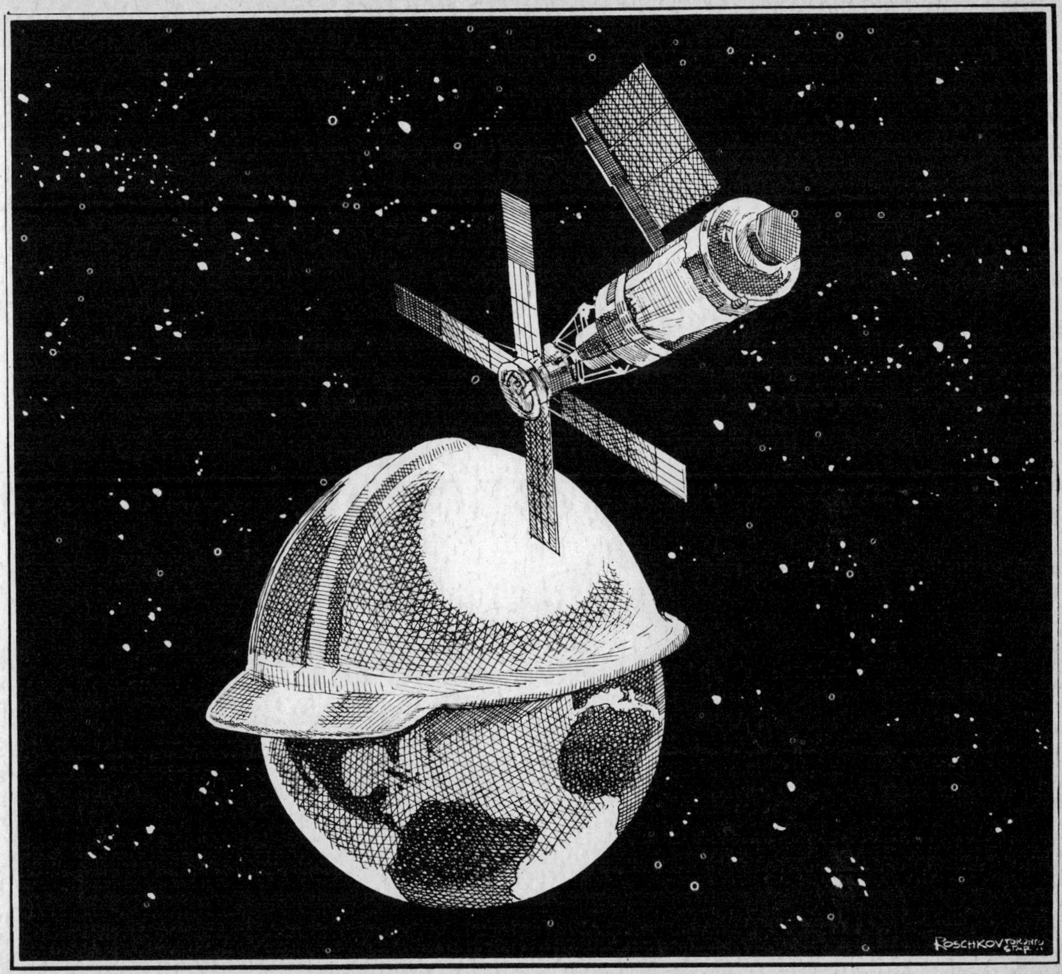
ROSCHKOV TORONTO STAR

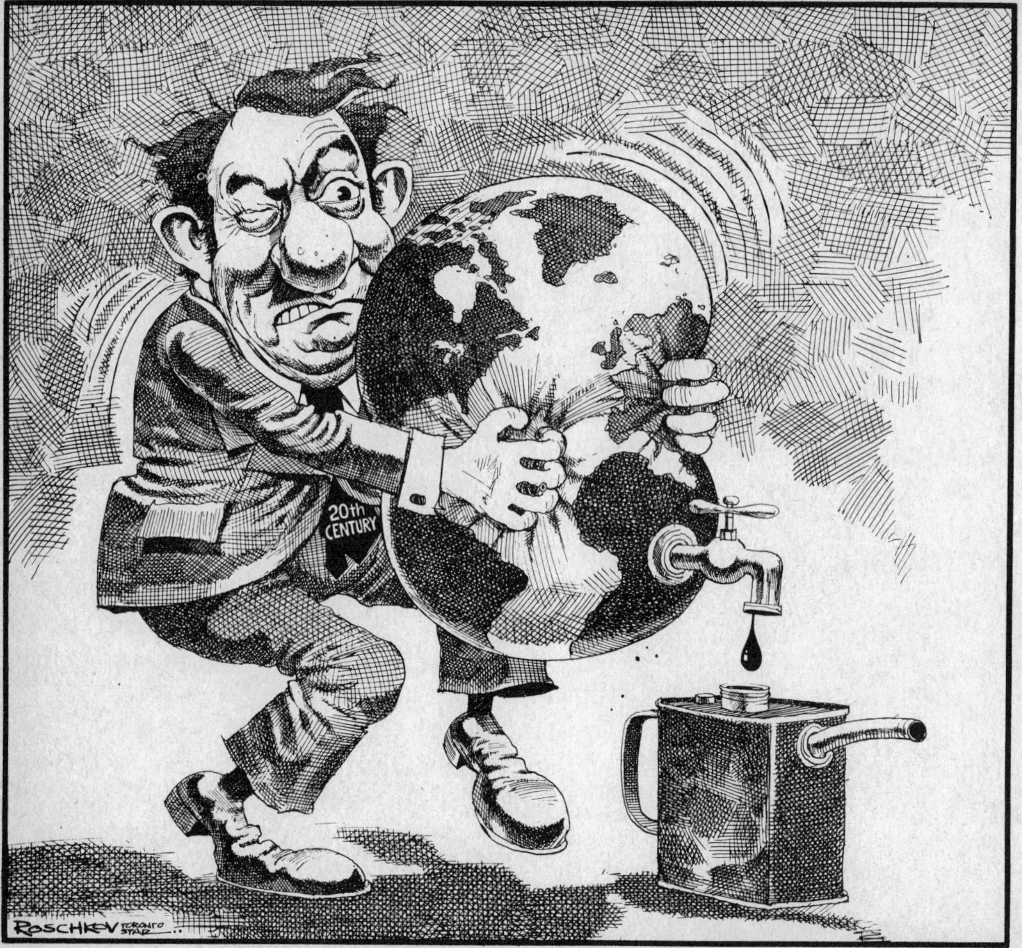
20th CENTURY
ROSCHKOV TORONTO STAR

"I'm, not in! Call Pierre..."

"The little lout—wants to buy back Canada.
By charging it on his American Express."

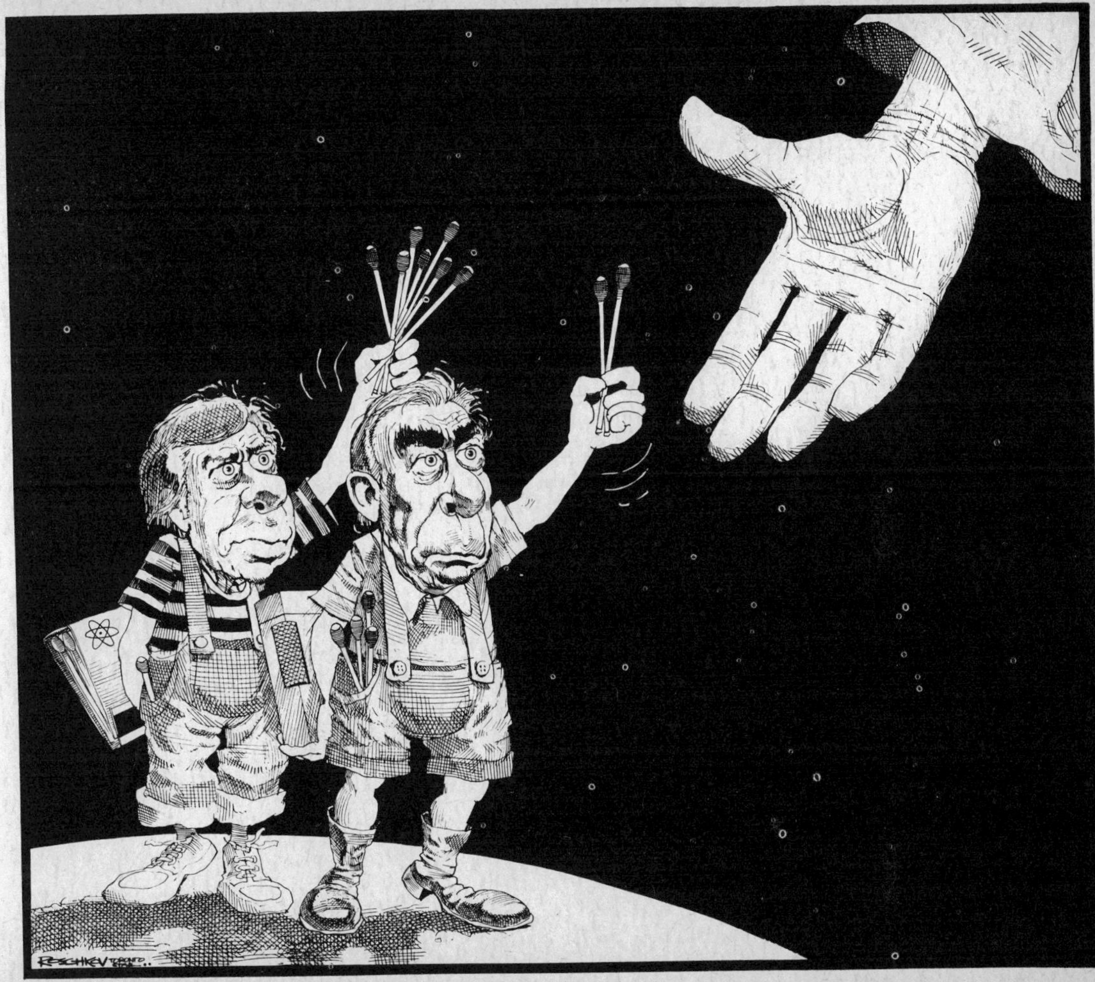
RESCHKEV

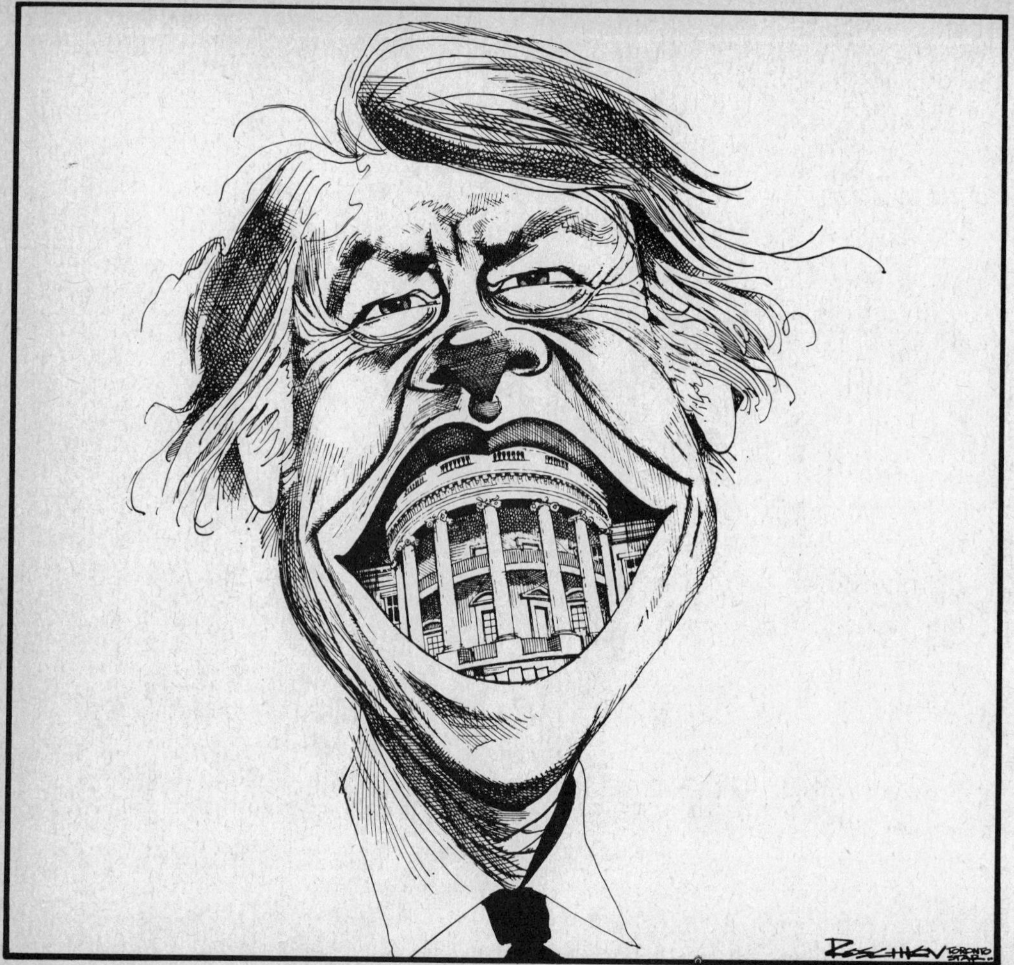

Blood for Allah

Government Austerity

YOU WANT TO QUIT THE TEAM _ BUT STILL REMAIN AS ITS RECEIVER ?
SURE _ THAT'S CALLED SOVEREIGNTY ASSOCIATION!
1
7
10
6
RESCHKOV

MORIN SUGGESTS JOINT PARLIAMENT WITH OTTAWA
ROSCHKOV
STAR

WEIRDO!
PROTEST THE SLAUGHTER OF PEOPLE IN SOUTHEAST ASIA
SPEAK OUT AGAINST THE SEAL HUNT
PRIORITIES INTERNATIONAL
SAVE
HE SEALS
CLUB A CANADIAN
STOP THE SLAUGHTER
CANADIANS ARE BARBARIANS
ROSCHKOV TORONTO STAR

"But wait a minute!
I'm from the same tribe..."

Winter '77

"Well, the demonstration worked— we got better living conditions..."

"Jumping Jack?"

BILL 101
ANGLAIS CANADA WE'VE GOT YOUR KID, ACCEPT OUR DEMANDS OR ELSE

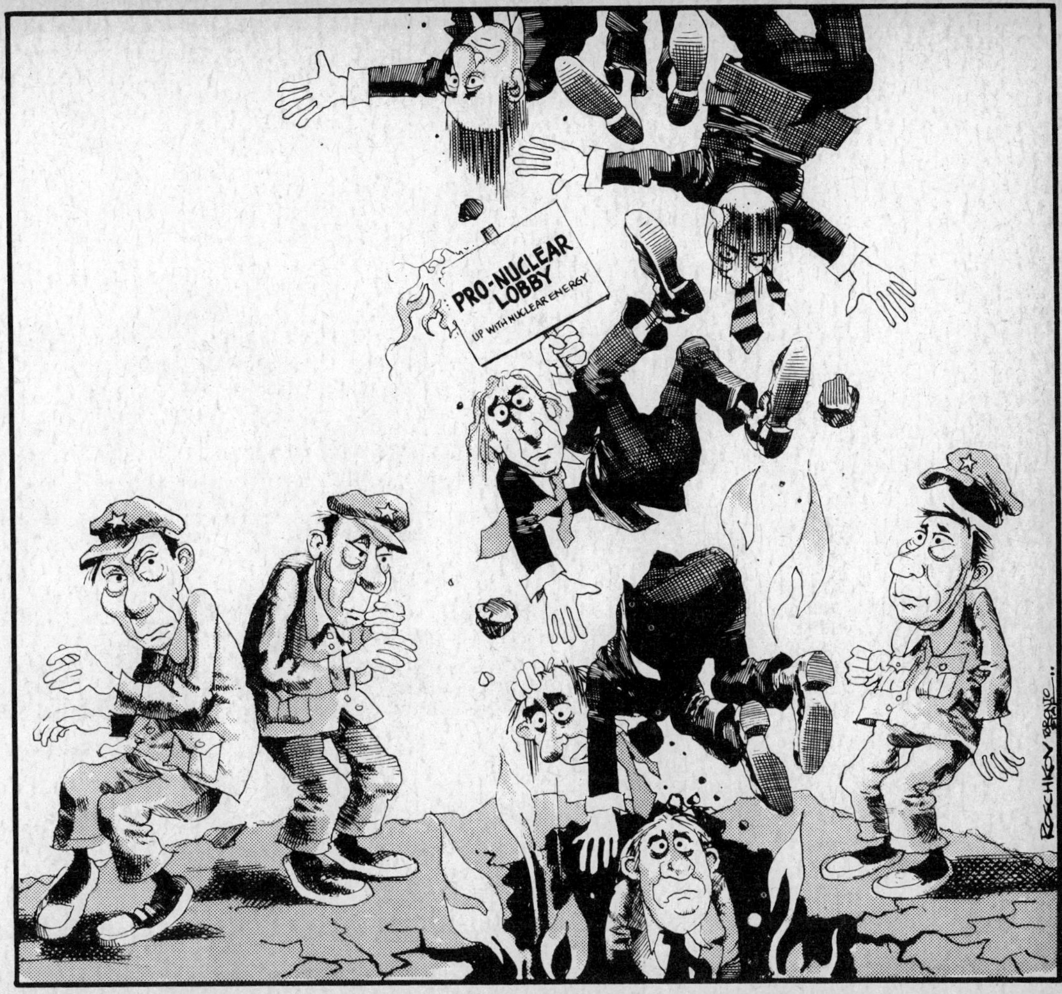
PRO-NUCLEAR LOBBY
UP WITH NUCLEAR ENERGY
ROSCHKOV

"What do they think we are, a bunch of animals?"

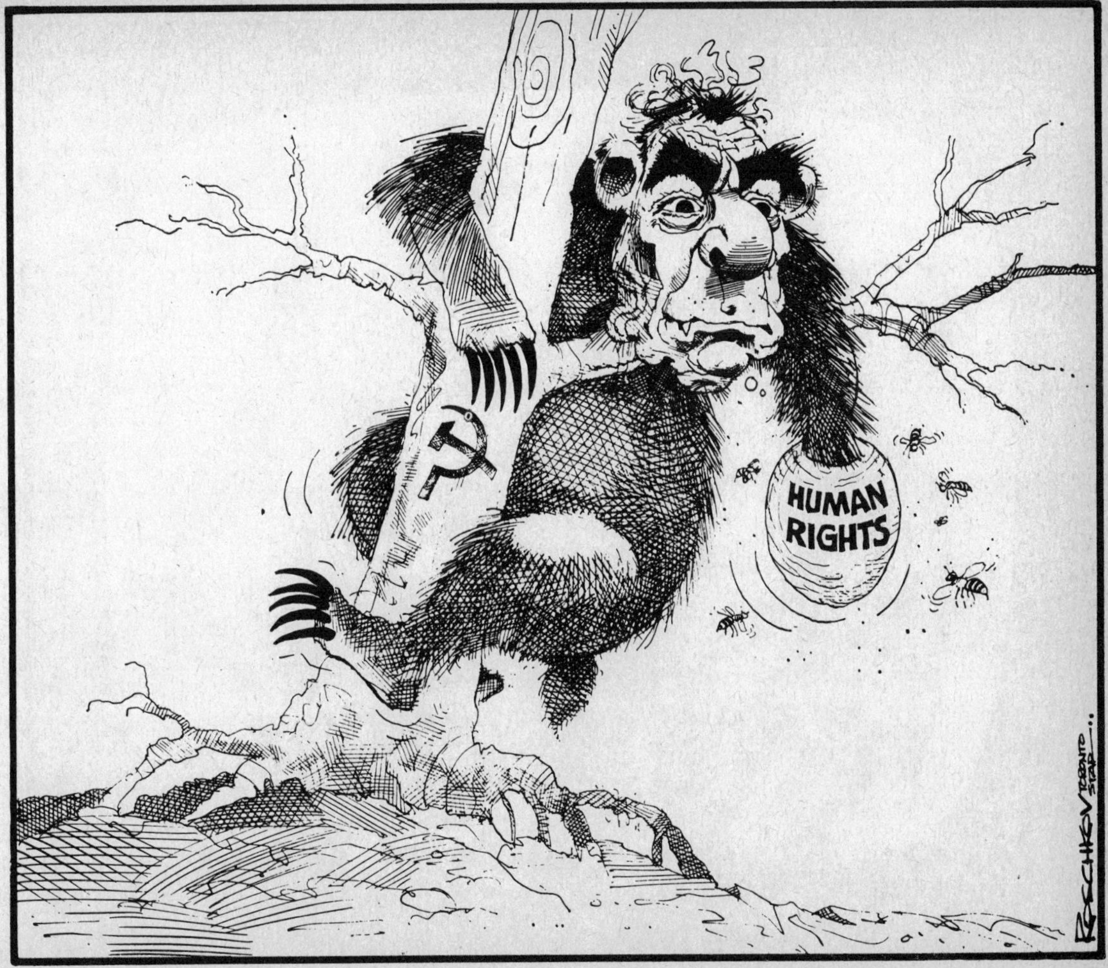
HUMAN RIGHTS

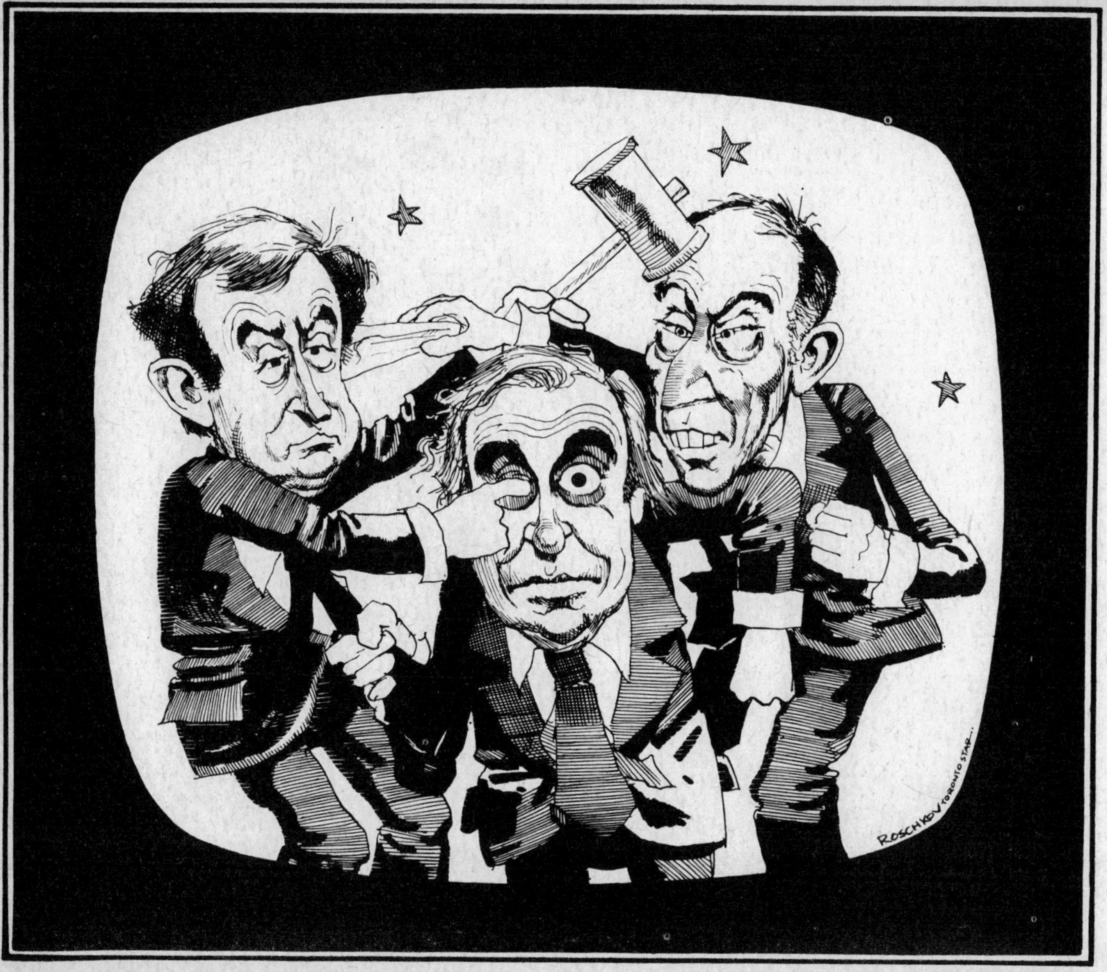
ROSCHKOV TORONTO STAR...

HOW DOES IT WORK?
WELL... AS THE DUCK COLLAPSES FROM AIR POLLUTION, IT FALLS OFF THE PLATFORM AND TRIGGERS THE SIREN TO ALERT EVERYONE OF THE DANGER..
WILL WE HAVE ENOUGH DUCKS?
ON
HERO
POLLUTION INDEX
ROSCHKOV WINDSOR STAR

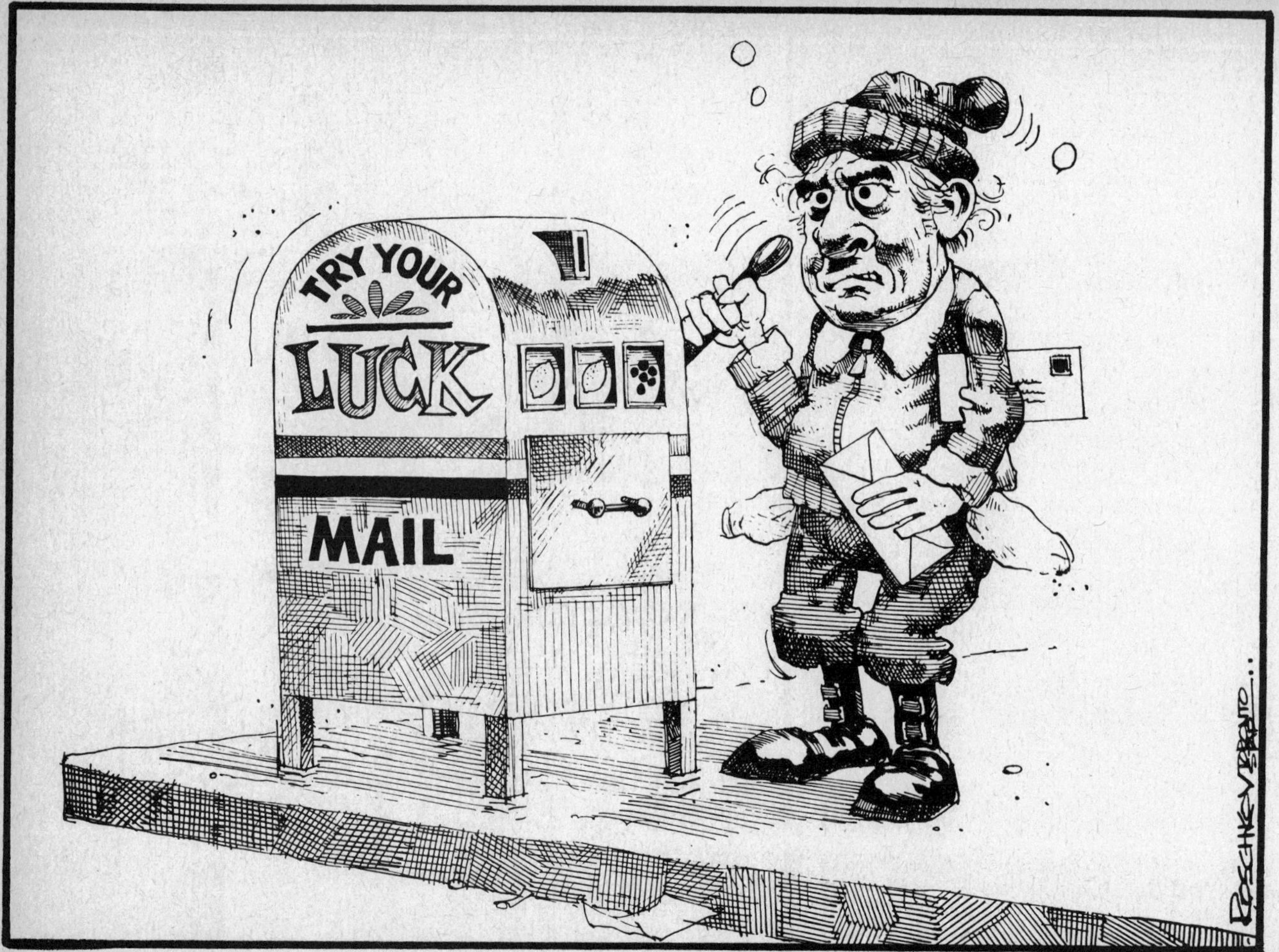
TRY YOUR
LUCK
MAIL

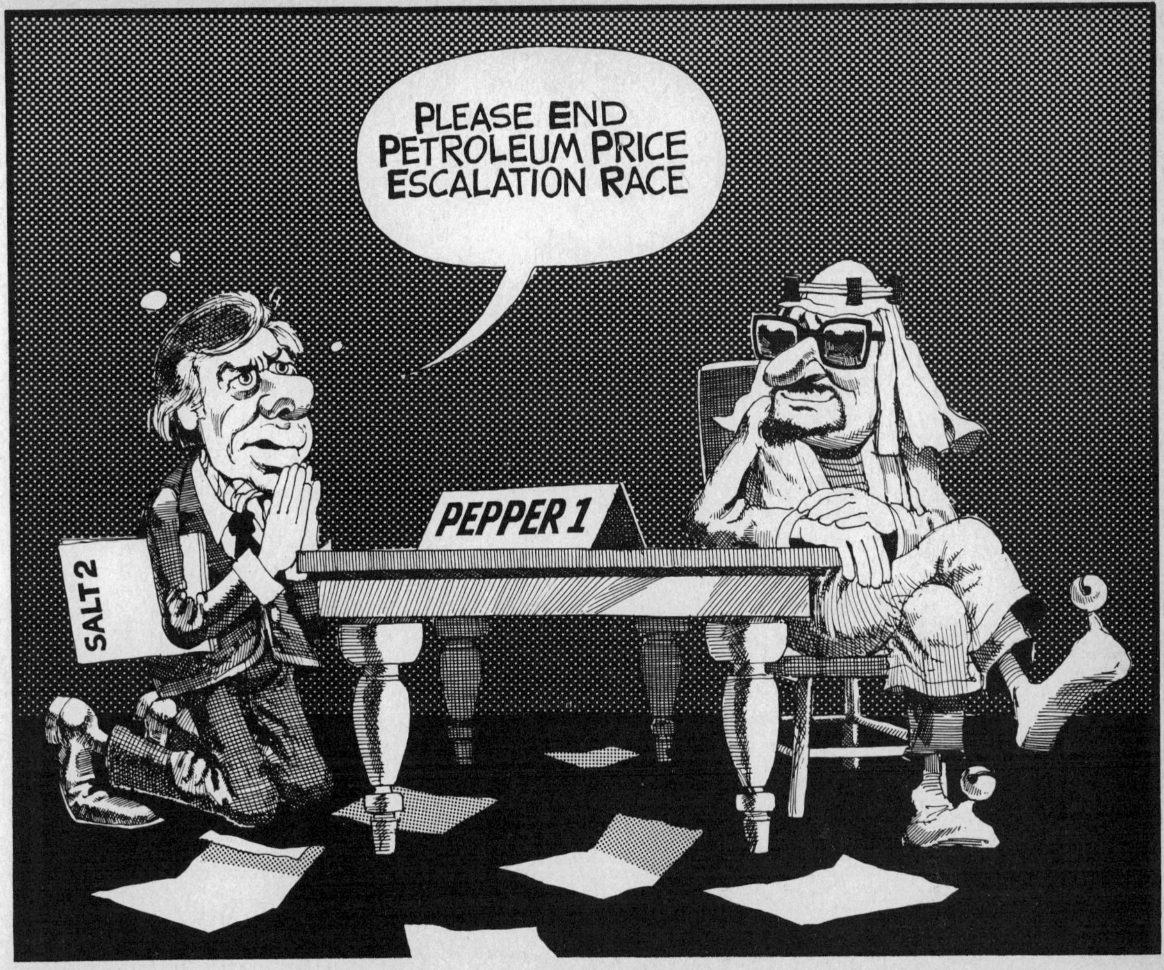
PLEASE END
PETROLEUM PRICE
ESCALATION RACE
PEPPER 1
SALT 2

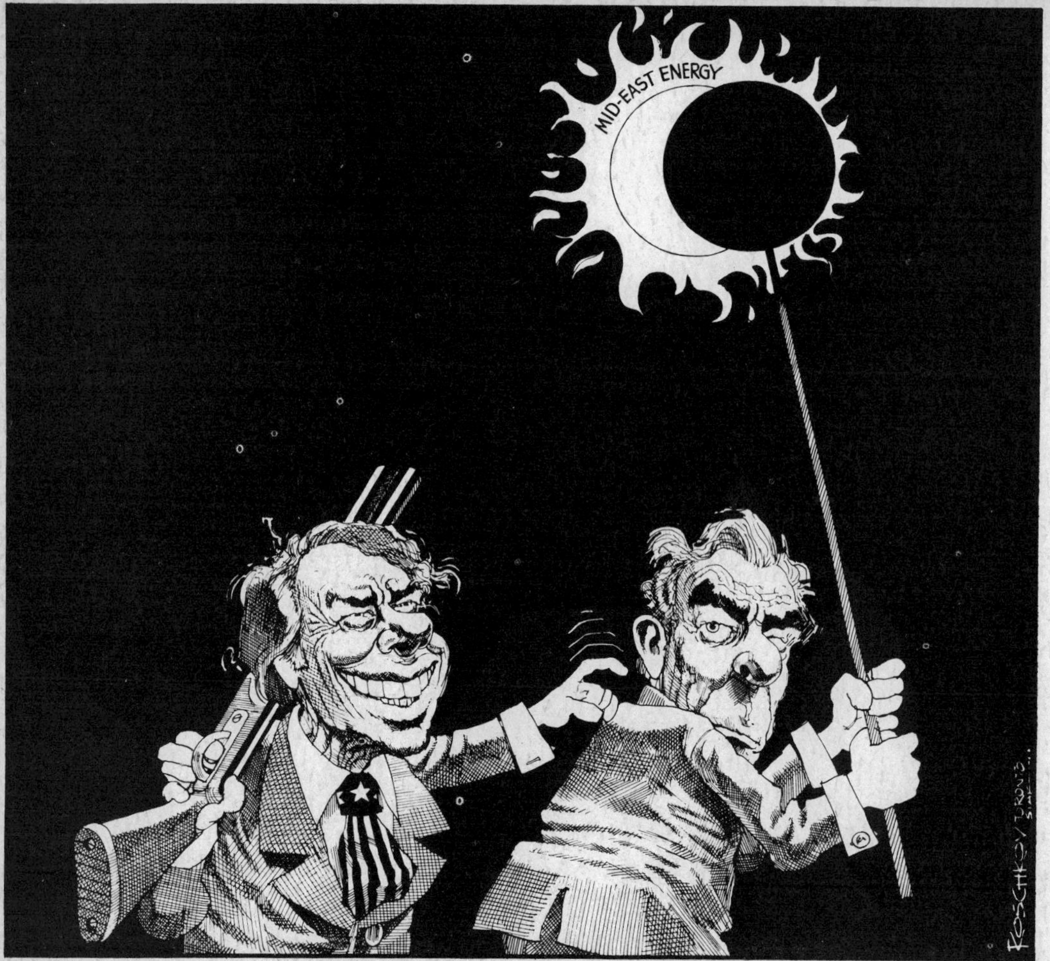
MID-EAST ENERGY

A REFERENDUM LIKE THE ONE IN BRITAIN
AN ECONOMIC ASSOCIATION SIMILAR TO THE EUROPEAN COMMON MARKET
SOCIAL DEMOCRACY ALONG THE LINES OF WEST GERMANY AND SWEDEN
AN AMERICAN-STYLE DECLARATION OF INDEPENDENCE
YOU KNOW, WHAT WE WANT IS OUR OWN IDENTITY
ROSCHKOV TORONTO STAR

Roschkov Toronto Star

Poison

HEY KEITH, MAYBE WE SHOULD BE RUNNING ON OUR RECORD?
JOBLESS RATE DROPS TO 7.9%
954,000 JOBLESS
JOE AND ED, ARE RUNNING ON OUR RECORD

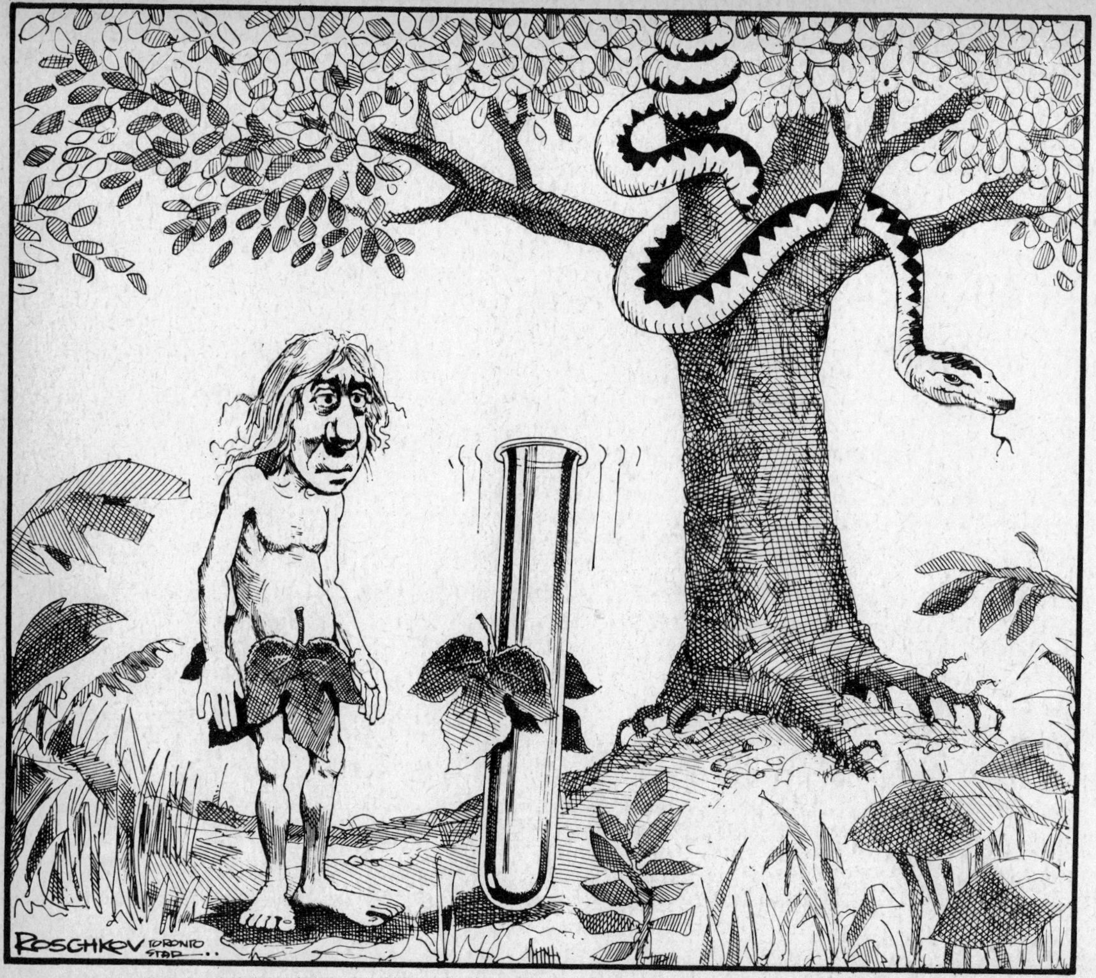
ROSCHKOV TORONTO STAR

"Here's your choice — acid rain, the risk of reactor melt-down or back to muscle power."

"Here's something to get our minds off mercury."

"Listen, Harry—you'll have to do those metric conversions quicker."

"Never mind the doomsayers— steady as she goes..."

"This democracy idea is getting out of control."

"I'm going to get all I can, before the meek inherit the earth."

We always get our man

From a little log cabin in High River . . .

TYRANT — A ruler unrestrained by law or constitution ... **WEBSTER'S**

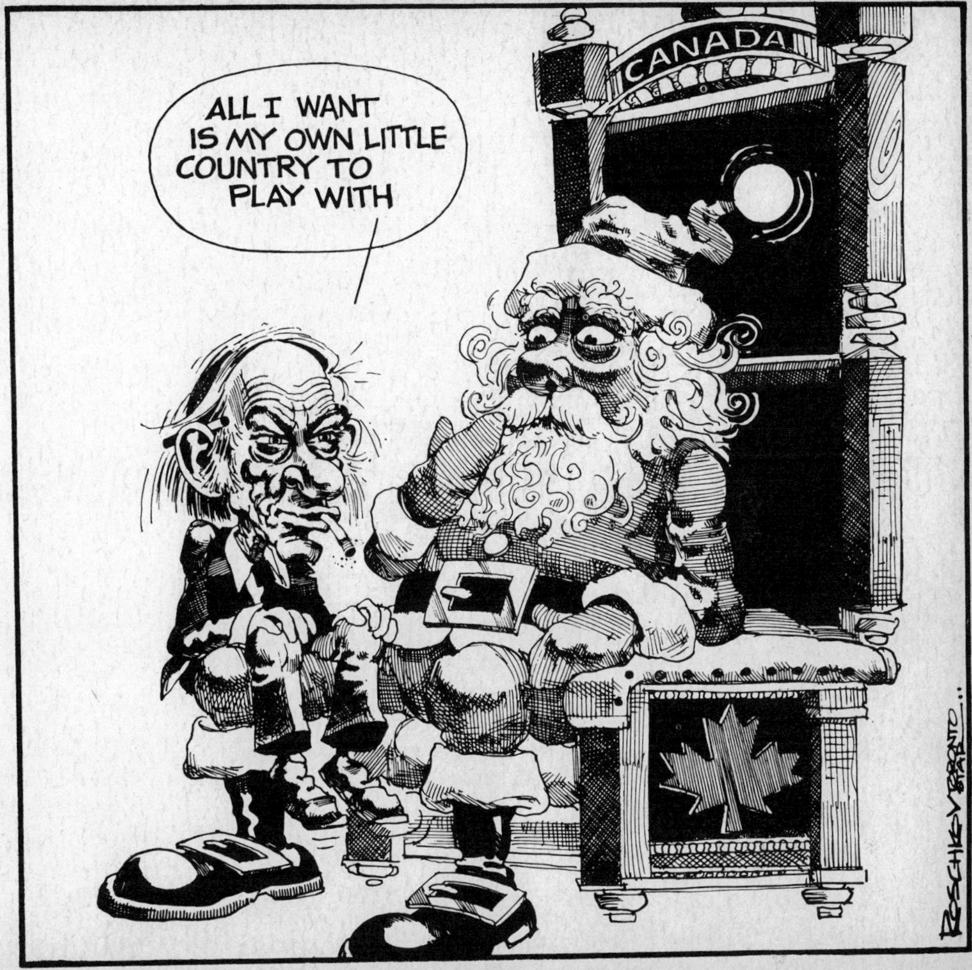
CANADA
ALL I WANT IS MY OWN LITTLE COUNTRY TO PLAY WITH

Peace Talks

Wrong Tune

"Our Fathers, Hail Marys...
How high can you count?"

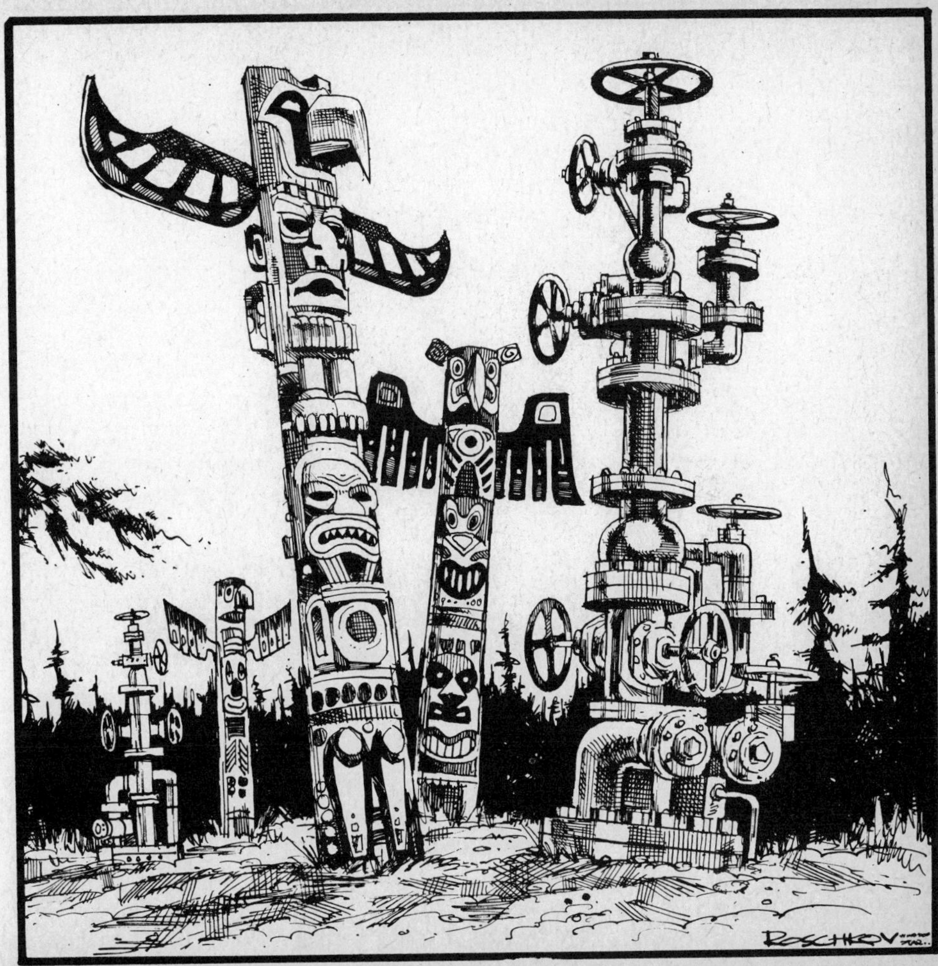
ROSCHKOV

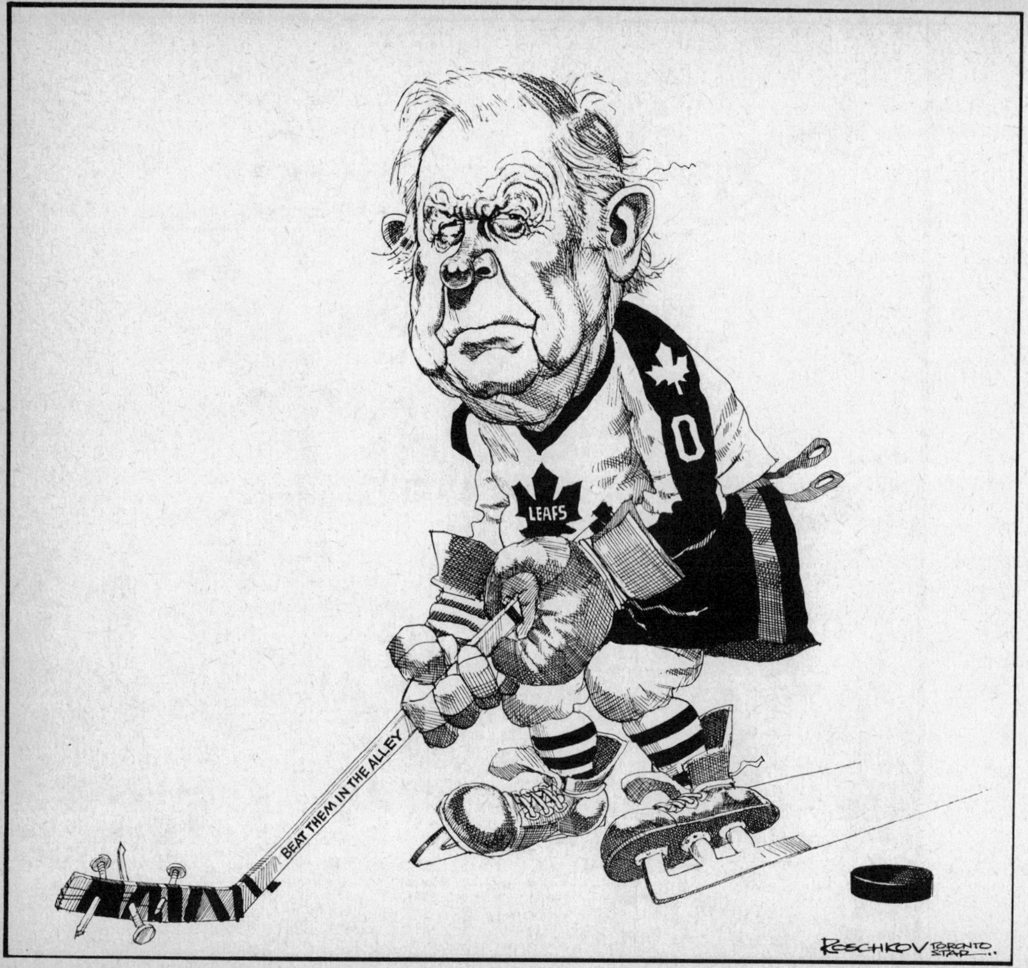

LEAFS
0
BEAT THEM IN THE ALLEY
ROSCHKOV TORONTO STAR

"They certainly were well groomed."

HOW'S THIS SOUND? THE SOVIET TRIAL CONTRAVENES THE SPIRIT OF HELSINKI, TO RESPECT HUMAN RIGHTS AND FUNDAMENTAL FREEDOMS
PETER TREU CASE
JAMIESON
ROSCHKOV TORONTO STAR

NEW YORK
SEPARATION
JC
OH CANADA
WASHINGTON
ROSCHKOV TORONTO STAR

Constitutional Summit

Remember when?

MAYBE I SHOULD HAVE LEFT THE SNAKES AND CHASED OUT THE IRISHMEN
ROSCHKOV
WINDSOR STAR

"Viva!"

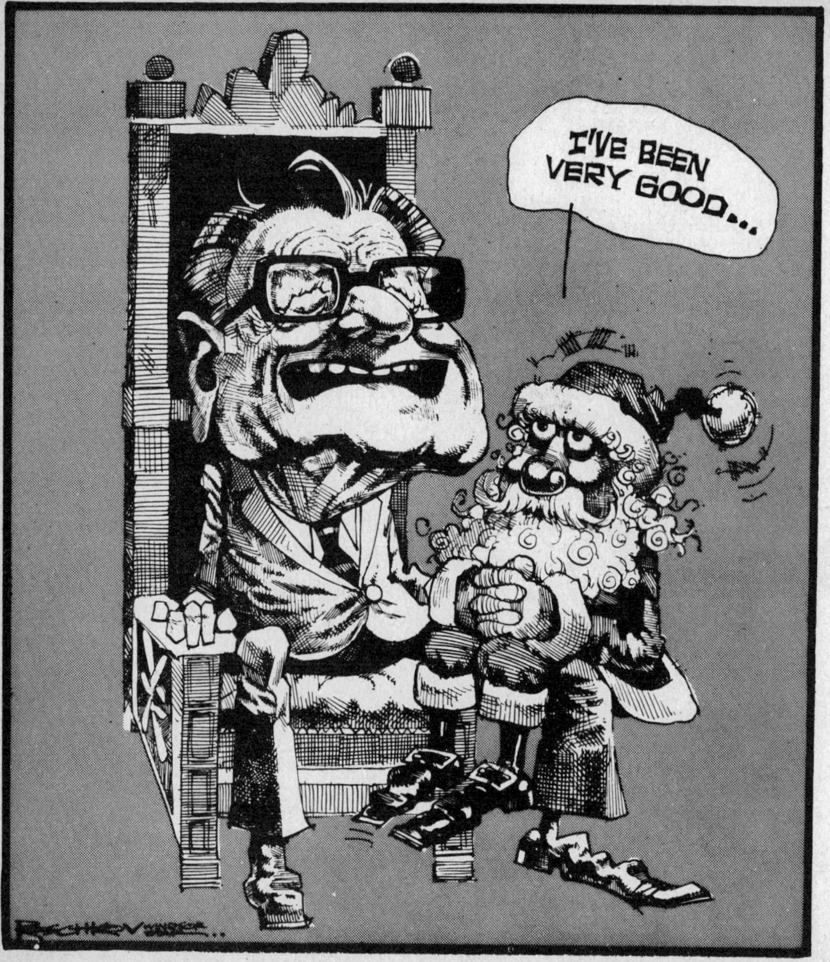
I'VE BEEN VERY GOOD...

TOMORROW STARTS TODAY— AND
TODAY IS THE DAY BEFORE TOMORROW.
ALTHOUGH THE DAY AFTER YESTERDAY
IS TODAY, YESTERDAY IS TWO DAYS
BEFORE TOMORROW AND ONE DAY
BEFORE TODAY. AND OF COURSE
THE DAY BEFORE TOMORROW IS
ALSO TODAY, BUT TOMORROW
IS THE DAY AFTER TODAY AND
TWO DAYS AFTER YESTERDAY...
NDP

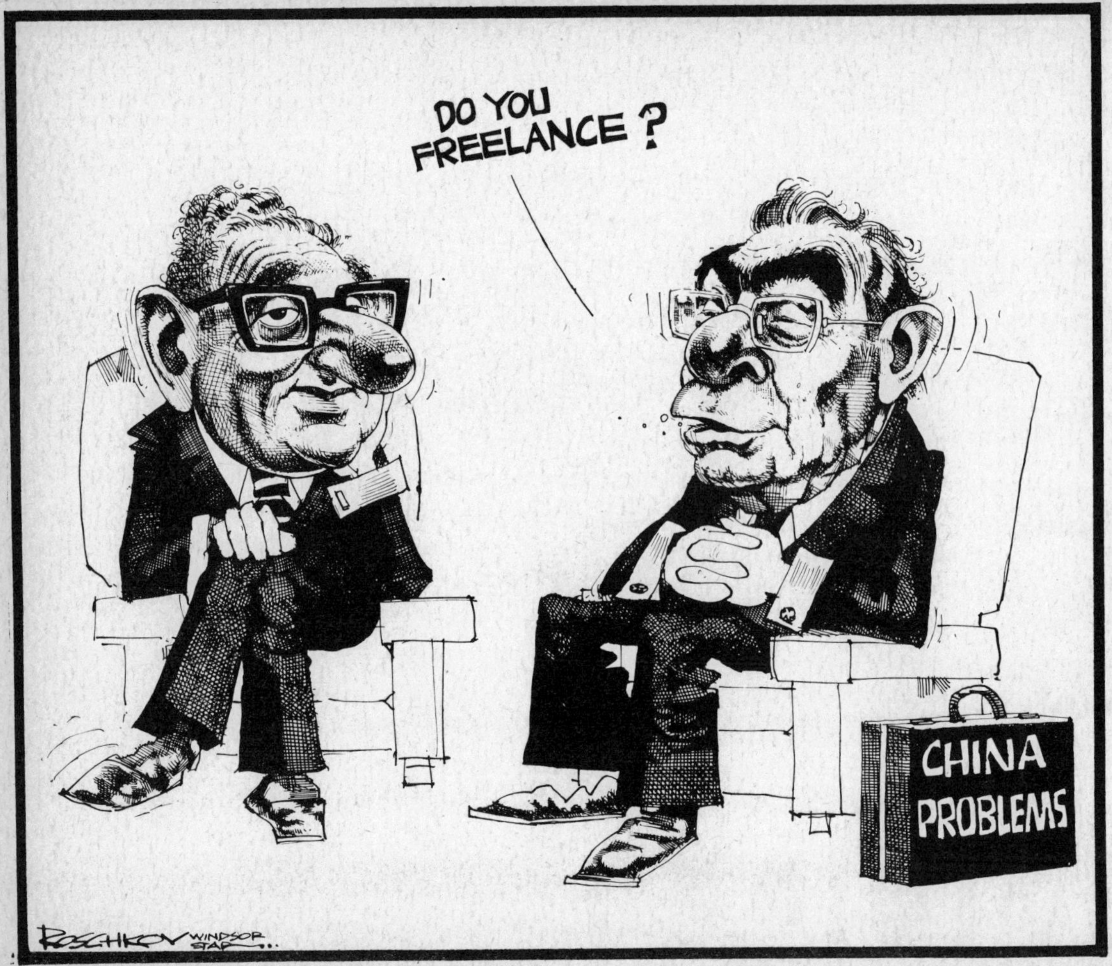
DO YOU
FREELANCE ?
CHINA
PROBLEMS
ROSCHKOV WINDSOR STAR

LINCOLN   FORD   EDSEL

PM boycotts plow competition because of Rhodesian participation

A victim of injustice?

"So far there is a strong indication of intelligent life, the craft hasn't been hijacked, we weren't refused entry for political reasons and there's no controversy about what language is safe in their air space..."

"Has anyone . . . hmmmm . . . click.
Ever --- hmmmm ... considered ..
blank . . . click -- that this is hhmmm ....
The way -- gap ..
. . . I sometimes -- hmmmm .. talk?"

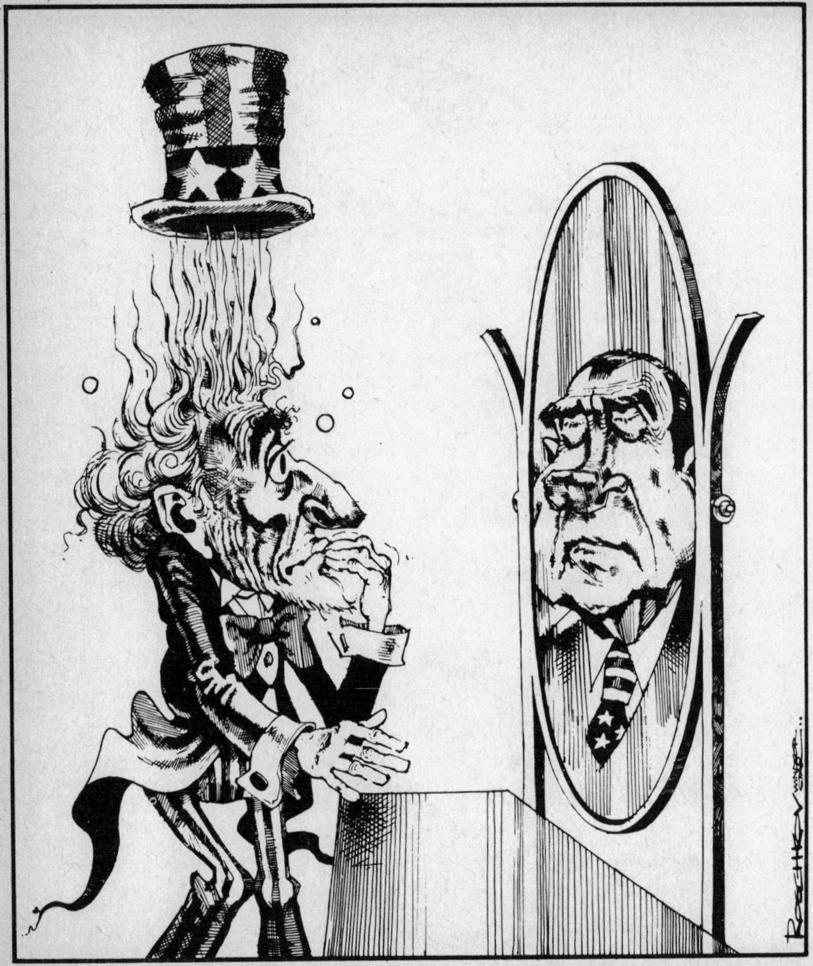

Drapeau Flop

I HOWARD HUGHES BEING OF SOUND MIND AND BODY LEAVE ALL MY BILLIONS TO JEAN DRAPEAU

"Let me be the first to wish you many, many more years in that distinguished position"